Acts of War

A Strategic Prayer Manual for Believers

By

Natassia K. Blassingame

Acts of War

A Strategic Prayer Manual for Believers

By

Natassia K. Blassingame

Worldwide Empowerment Center
Natassia Blassingame
PO Box 465
Blandon, Pennsylvania 19510
USA
www.actsofwar1.com

Acts of War

A Strategic Prayer Manual for Believers

ISBN 13 TP: 978-1-962808-09-5

ISBN 13 eBook: 978-1-962808-10-1

Cover Design by Darian Horner Design

(www.darianhorner.com)

Image: elements.envato.com AT6TJPB

Table of Contents

Dedication and Thanks

This book is dedicated to God, my everything. Thank you for trusting me. Special thanks to my husband, my children, my sister Icelyn, my editor, and my publishing company, may God's blessings always be with you.

Introduction

Many people pray, yet often find the answers they seek elusive. As a passionate advocate for those seeking to deepen their prayer lives, I've created this unique *prayer manual*. It's not just another resource on prayer; it's a comprehensive guide for those eager to learn how to pray and where to begin. Moreover, it serves as a valuable reference for those advancing in their authority in Christ Jesus. This manual doesn't just reiterate the basics; it propels the reader to a new level of prayer.

In a world rife with fear, anxiety, and worry, many yearn for guidance on how to pray and integrate prayer into their daily lives. This manual serves as a beacon of hope, enhancing the meaning and value of prayer and equipping readers with the tools to confront challenging situations.

While some view prayer as merely petitioning, engaging in spiritual warfare, or intercession only, it is much more than that. We are soldiers in the army of the Lord, each equipped with unique spiritual weapons to fight the enemy. This manual is designed to be practical and applicable to everyday life, with tools and suggestions to help the believer accomplish much in battle. It also fosters a strong sense of community and shared purpose, reminding the reader we are not alone in this fight. We are not alone in this fight.

This manual will help readers understand that everything God has given us through Jesus Christ is a weapon we can use in any situation. My goal is to provide a framework for understanding what it means to engage in a spiritual battle against the works of Satan. Having the clarity that the enemy Satan and those who he uses must submit to the finished work of Jesus Christ in the earth which has been left to the believer to govern and enforce.

Chapter 1

Why Pray

The Bible serves as the primary way through which God communicates with us, while prayer stands as the primary way we communicate with God. Additionally, prayer is a potent weapon of warfare. When we pray the heart, will, and the Word of God, it destroys the spiritual attacks directed against us.

Prayer is a powerful weapon for humbling ourselves before God and seeking His help. It is a believer's way of submitting to God and acknowledging dependence on Him. Regular prayer is not just a habit but a lifestyle that brings stability and certainty to our lives. By intentionally devoting time to prayer and developing discipline in it, we shape our lives and experiences. Remember that what we give time and attention to will grow. So, if you invest in prayer, you will reap the benefits of a strengthened prayer life.

Prayer is an essential part of a believer's spiritual development. It guides us to discover our identity and direction in an active reality where Jesus Christ is Lord. Through prayer, our destiny can be revealed, allowing us to understand our true selves by knowing who God designed us to be. When facing life's challenges, prayer proves to be an effective weapon to address the needs of our spirit, soul, and body. Our identity and purpose, as planned by God, have been under attack since the beginning of time. Prayer serves as a means to reclaim what the enemy has stolen from us in any battle.

The Value of Prayer

Prayer holds profound power to unveil fundamental truths. As God's creation, it is essential to earnestly desire and seek Him, acknowledging His sovereignty and choosing Him above all else. Our battle extends beyond worldly conflicts; we also see attacks on our relationship with God, inner peace, joy, happiness, and the truth of who we are. As believers, responding to this spiritual warfare through prayer is essential.

Prayer is the act of conversing directly with God, not merely contemplation or meditation. It is important to understand how to pray. It involves making requests to God, as exemplified when Jesus' disciples asked Him to teach them to pray (Luke 11:1). Effective prayer requires learning and seeking guidance.

To pray effectively, one must communicate with God, be led by the Holy Spirit, be consistent and persistent in prayer, and submit to His will. Prayer is also a legal petition—a demand made on the government by its citizens. Jesus Christ established the governing authority of God on earth as it is in Heaven. We are citizens of Heaven (Philippians 3:20), and we are seated in heavenly places in Christ Jesus (Ephesians 2:6). We no longer need what we obtained from this world because it is not viable in this fight.

Prayer is not weariness, desperation, bargaining, IOUs, or a promissory note reserved for certain individuals or intercessors; it is for everyone. It fosters unity and oneness between believers and God, employing diverse strategies to overcome opposition, challenges, and personal battles rooted in the spiritual realm. These strategies require the believer to possess the knowledge, wisdom, revelation, and truth needed to wield the weapons to overcome.

Take a moment to reflect on why you pray and what you have learned about prayer. Would you still pray if you faced no obstacles in life? Would you still seek God if your desires were fulfilled and you had everything you wanted? Would you choose to seek God if you didn't need Him? These questions prompt a deeper examination of our relationship with Him.

Scriptures on Prayer

- **1 Thessalonians 5:16-18:** Rejoice always, pray without ceasing, in everything give thanks; for this is the will of God in Christ Jesus for you.

- **Ephesians 6:18 (MSG):** With all prayer and petition, pray [with specific requests] at all times [on every occasion and in every season] in the Spirit, and with this in view, stay alert with all perseverance and petition [interceding in prayer] for all God's people.

- **Matthew 6:5-8:** And when you pray, you shall not be like the hypocrites. For they love to pray standing in the synagogues and on the corners of the streets, that they may be seen by men. Assuredly, I say to you, they have their reward. But you, when you pray, go into your room, and when you have shut your door, pray to your Father who is in the secret place; and your Father who sees in secret will reward you openly. And when you pray, do not use vain repetitions as the heathen do. For they think that they will be heard for their many words. Therefore, do not be like them. For your Father knows the things you need before you ask Him.

Honoring Him as King

Before entering God's presence to pray, it's important to honor him as King of Kings and Lord of Lords. His sovereignty should be worshiped with thanksgiving and praise. These three preparations are needed to bring you into God's presence and provide a starting point for engaging in spiritual warfare.

1. **Worship:** A sacred practice involving calling upon God's name, seeking His presence through song, dance, the raising of hands, and showing deep reverence and respect.
2. **Thanksgiving:** Joyfully expressing gratitude and praise to God for the abundance of blessings received.
3. **Praise:** Recognizing and honoring God for the amazing things He has accomplished, giving Him the honor He deserves.

These three preparations bring you into God's presence. Then, you can begin with the prayer of adoration, thanksgiving, confession, vows, quiet reflection, healing, deliverance, help, intercession, transformation, blessings, judgment, and warfare.

The Rules of Engagement

What is required in prayer? Knowing the rules of engagement is a requirement of any war. We will use common military terms to clarify our roles as soldiers in the army of the Lord.

Rules of engagement in the military are directives meant to describe the circumstances under which ground, naval, and air forces will enter and continue combat with opposing forces. Formally, *rules of engagement*[1] refer to the orders issued by a competent military authority that delineate when, where, how, and against whom military force may be used, and they have implications for what actions soldiers may take on their authority and what directives may be issued by a commanding officer. Rules of engagement are part of a general recognition that procedures and standards are essential to the conduct and effectiveness of civilized warfare.

---

[1] "Rules of Engagement," *Encyclopaedia Britannica*, last modified August 14, 2024, https://www.britannica.com/topic/economic-warfare.

- As believers, we must consider the rules of engagement in prayer. The blood of the Lamb has saved us. The price of redemption was the life of Jesus Christ, the Son of God. Since we have been bought for a price, we have been adopted and now receive an inheritance that restores authority and power to the believer.

- Procedures and standards are essential to the conduct and effectiveness of your prayers. Your success in prayer depends on you utilizing the correct directives given by the Holy Spirit, who, in this example, would represent your commanding officer. If you are not engaging the Holy Spirit with the authority given to you by Christ Jesus in natural and supernatural situations, you can never win the battle. Romans 8:14-17 says,

> For as many as are led by the Spirit of God, these are sons of God. For you did not receive the spirit of bondage again to fear, but you received the Spirit of adoption by whom we cry out, "Abba, Father." The Spirit Himself bears witness with our spirit that we are children of God, and if children, then heirs— heirs of God and joint heirs with Christ, if indeed we suffer

7

with Him, that we may also be glorified together.

- We also receive access to Heaven as joint heirs in Christ. We are seated in heavenly places in Christ Jesus. This means that the finished work of Christ is in the earth and the heavens.

- As believers, we must acquaint ourselves with God's instructions and orders to humanity and the teachings left by Jesus Christ. According to the Bible, God created humanity to be fruitful, multiply, fill the earth, subdue it, and have dominion over it. Additionally, Jesus Christ has granted us the authority to trample over the power of all the enemies on the earth. We have access to Heaven through the redemption of Christ's blood.

- We have been granted access in the natural and spirit realm to the heavenly hosts of angels on land, sea, and air to overcome opposition. Psalms 91:11 tells us that He shall give His angels charge over you, to keep you in all your ways.

- Every situation, trial, or tribulation requires a different prayer strategy and response. To know the requirements for the specific attack, you must know your opponent and what proper, legal, or illegal accusation they have to bring a war against you. The enemy Satan is always looking to bring an accusation against the believer. He is the accuser of the brethren; his focus is to find a way to kill, steal, and destroy you, your destiny, and everyone connected to you.

- It's common to think that leaving the devil alone will prevent him from attacking us. However, this is not true. Satan will always be our enemy because we are the sons of God. Therefore, we must realize our position as God's children and carry out His will. When Jesus Christ died on the cross, He gained all power and authority in Heaven and Earth. The same Holy Spirit that raised Jesus from the dead now dwells within us, giving us the power to live out God's plan for our lives.

Optimizing Prayer

Getting the most out of prayer will require you to:

1. Read your Bible daily, asking God for understanding, revelation, and illumination of what is written. Rightly handle the word of truth (2 Timothy 2:15).

2. Meditate on the Word of God daily so that you may recall it at any time for strength and direction (Psalms 119:7-8).

3. Memorize scriptures from the Bible that build your faith, unlock your identity, and speak the promises and blessings of God for you (Psalms 119:11; Colossians 3:16).

4. Speak the Word of God by believing it is true. Be confident in the authority and power given to you through the Holy Spirit (Isaiah 55:11; Mark 11:24).

5. Stand on the Word of God with confidence; it is the foundation of your belief system (2 Timothy 3:16-17).

Prayer is a significant means of communication with God and a powerful tool for spiritual warfare. By dedicating time to prayer regularly and developing discipline in it, we can transform our lives and experiences. Effective prayer requires being led by the Holy Spirit, communicating with God, and submitting to His will. As believers, we have access to the Holy Spirit, heavenly hosts of angels, and Christ's authority to fulfill God's plan for our lives.

Chapter 2

What is Not Often Known About Prayer

For a long time, I struggled with prayer. I had only two go-to prayers: The Lord's Prayer (from Matthew 6), which Jesus taught His disciples, and King Solomon's prayer (in 1 Kings 3) for wisdom, knowledge, and understanding.

While these prayers were powerful, they didn't always reflect my heart in extreme situations. I felt a fleeting sense of peace, but I wasn't confident that God heard my prayer. This was because I knew that my life and choices didn't always reflect God's will for me. I believed that my prayer was only heard if my life looked like those of other faithful people. However, I now understand that God loves us all with everlasting love. He doesn't judge us through our limited perspectives. That's why it's important to invite God into our situations through prayer. Before doing so, we need to be aware of some fundamental truths.

The Truth About the Rules

It is not widely known that certain prerequisites must be met before requesting anything in prayer. Failure to meet these requirements can result in misguided prayers. Have you ever prayed to God and not received what you asked for? Do you still seek answers to a request you have brought to God? We have all experienced this at some point.

There are many factors to consider when praying, and the specific rules that apply to a particular prayer request are often unknown. Many people believe that asking in Jesus' name is the key to unlocking the door to our petitions. However, there are many keys to different doors that can lead to answers for each situation.

Keys to Answered Prayers

- The first key should be to stop and ask God what He wants or is doing in the specific problem we are praying about.
- We must be adequately equipped with understanding to pray by speaking, knowing, and believing the truth

of who we are in the Kingdom of God and who God is in His sovereignty.

- We must stand firm in the Lord and His mighty power. This war is not against your flesh and blood but your identity in Christ Jesus. So, the battle must be won by fighting with the weapons God gave us. We have access because of the blood of Christ Jesus.

- The Holy Spirit provides us with the power to fight against the rulers, against the authorities, against the powers of this dark world, and the spiritual forces of evil in the heavenly realms.

- Because we are believers of Christ and given full access to His inheritance, we can come as a witness with access to Heaven and on Earth in full possession of the keys of the Kingdom of Heaven; whatever we bind on earth will be bound in Heaven, and whatever we loose on Earth will be loosed in Heaven, according to Matthew 16:19.

Standing In the Truth as Sons

We must begin to stand in our complete authority as sons of God. The Word of God is faithful; the effectiveness of the Word depends on your ability to live and be led by it. The following are absolute truths that we can stand in as sons:

1. We are citizens of Heaven, and our identity is in Christ Jesus.

Only Jesus Christ could accomplish what was done on Earth. His blood is the payment for all sins of humanity, allowing us to be both on Earth and in heavenly places. As believers, we now rule and reign with Christ Jesus and have access to commune with God so that everything on the earth must submit to His Lordship. Because Jesus Christ is Lord, He allows us to establish His will on Earth.

As citizens of Heaven, we don't have to wait until we die to use what we have been given. We can agree with the Holy Spirit, who reveals the mysteries of God. The Holy Spirit should lead, guide, and direct us in all aspects of our citizenship in Heaven.

> For our citizenship is in heaven, from which we also eagerly wait for the Savior, the Lord Jesus Christ, who will transform our lowly body that it may be conformed to His glorious body, according to the working by which He is able even to subdue all things to Himself. (Philippians 3:20-21)

2. We are ambassadors of Heaven to the earth.

As ambassadors, we reflect Christ on Earth and represent our place of origin—Heaven. Being image bearers of God, we are to fulfill His desires. If you identify as a Christian, you submit to the authority of Jesus and accept His lordship over your life.

> *Now then, we are ambassadors for Christ, as though God were pleading through us: we implore you, on Christ's behalf, be reconciled to God. For He made Him who knew no sin to be sin for us, that we might become the righteousness of God in Him. (2 Corinthians 5:20-21)*

3. We are ministers of reconciliation.

To become a minister of reconciliation, we must first accept the assignment. This requires you to let go of your desires and agendas and allow God to mold you into the design He intends for you. We are to be the accurate example and representation of reconciliation. God's ultimate desire is for humanity to fulfill His purpose, and He does not want anyone to be lost. He sent His only begotten Son to pay for humanity's sins. He wants every person to be saved, but for that to happen, the truth must be shared. We have been made ministers of reconciliation, and through Christ, we have been reconciled back to God.

> *Now all things are of God, who has reconciled us to Himself through Jesus Christ, and has given us the ministry of reconciliation, that is, that God was in Christ reconciling the world to Himself, not imputing their trespasses to them, and has committed to us the word of reconciliation. (2 Corinthians 5:18-19)*

4. The truth is that we are children of God to whom Jesus has given authority over all the enemy's power.

The agenda of any soldier in battle is to gain ground, win territory, and remove opposition. The most important truth we must understand is that we are not powerless. Whenever we believe that we are helpless against a situation or circumstance, that situation or circumstance will completely control us. Instead, we need to turn to the truth that tells us that we are children of God to whom Jesus has given authority over all the enemy's power.

Whatever we face in life requires a necessary response to address it. The Holy Spirit is the only way to identify the correct weapon for the challenge. The Word of God is the most essential weapon to use in the battle against the enemy's powers. Any other means of gaining victory over a problem or situation is outside of God's original intent and is illegal. Jesus Christ is the authority we have been given to establish change on Earth according to how it is in Heaven. We must establish the true intent of God through Christ Jesus to witness victory in every situation. If we let our mind, will, or emotions determine how we respond to problems and challenges, we are essentially showing up to a battle with no armor and no way of gaining an upper hand in prayer.

> But as many as received Him, to them He gave the right to become children of God, to those who believe in His name: who were born, not of blood, nor the will of the flesh, nor of the will of man, but of God. (John 1:12-13)

> But you shall receive power when the Holy Spirit has come upon you, and you shall be witnesses to Me in Jerusalem, and in all Judea and Samaria, and to the end of the earth. (Acts 1:8)

The authority of Jesus Christ enforces the will of God in our hearts through our prayers. His sacrifice on the cross cannot be denied, so we must stand in that truth.

5. We must get up and get dressed!

We must stay alert, in proper garments, with the whole armor of God on so that we stand against the devil's schemes.

This is a defensive position that we should apply daily. The truth is that the whole armor of God is found in the righteousness of God. His righteousness is the foundation upon which we stand. Just like a soldier cannot wear armor without foundational pieces, living in Christ Jesus clothes us in righteousness and forgiveness, and we are no longer naked and ashamed. The Bible speaks of the effects of sin, which makes our garments filthy, and the need for them to be changed or cleaned. The scriptures also mention the garment of praise, salvation, and righteousness, which are essential for the believer to maintain by examining themselves frequently.

The whole armor of God is applied over the foundational garment of righteousness and forgiveness given to us by Christ Jesus. Wearing this armor requires spiritual strength; we must be spiritually fit to bear its weight. To stay in shape, we need to be obedient, repentant, willing to sacrifice, be disciplined and agree with the will of God. Our battle is spiritual, against principalities, powers, authorities of the unseen world, mighty powers in the dark world, and evil spirits in the heavenly realms. God desires that we resist the enemy in times of evil, and after the battle is finished, we stand firmly in our armor.

This armor includes the belt of truth, the breastplate of righteousness, the sandals of the gospel of peace, the shield of faith, and the helmet of salvation. We must always carry the Word of God in our hearts. The final piece to our armor is prayer which is often forgotten and frequently overlooked. The believer must pray in the Holy Spirit on all occasions with all kinds of prayers and requests. With this in mind, be alert and always keep on praying for all the Lord's people.

Our actions should include prayer, supplication, decreeing, declaring, repentance, and applying the blood of Jesus Christ.

In battle, believers must remember to wear the correct armor and use the right weapons. For example, David declined King Saul's armor to fight the giant Philistine Goliath. David knew he could only succeed with what had brought him previous victories.

It's imperative to have access to weapons of warfare to effect change in our surroundings, families, and homes. Equally important is understanding how to use them effectively and responsibly. Gathering information and accessing all the tools and weapons that God has bestowed upon us is crucial.

Therefore, it's necessary to understand spiritual warfare and apply it in a spiritual battle. We have access to the armor of truth, righteousness, and peace, to name a few.

Wearing the whole armor of God allows believers to present the gospel truthfully.

Before each battle, it's crucial to inspect our armor thoroughly. What happens when the armor we wear has been breached or weakened? This could leave us vulnerable to the enemy's attacks. In war, after a battle, many soldiers take the time to inspect their armor to guarantee that its integrity is intact. Without this process, our armor can be susceptible to the enemy's penetration and cause a fatal outcome.

Regular inspection of your armor involves having rest, reflection, and deep repentance periods. Only a person who relies on the sovereignty of God can see and hear His will and plan. Another way to examine your armor is by ensuring that your spirit, soul, and body are in proper submission after the battle. The believer can identify if there is a crack in the helmet, a bullet lodged in the breastplate, a hole in any shoe, a defect in the belt buckle, a dull sword that needs to be sharpened, or a dent in the shield. These references are symbolic of any area of our life that has not been surrendered to God.

The armor described in the Bible represents various aspects of living a righteous life in the truth of God. It symbolizes protection through righteousness, a peaceful walk, using faith as a shield, and the Holy Spirit's governance of our thoughts, will, and emotions (Ephesians 6:11-13).

Different types of armor, such as the Armor of Light (Romans 13:12) and the Armor of Righteousness (2 Corinthians 6:7), serve specific purposes in believers' lives. The breastplate of faith and love and the hope of salvation as a helmet (1 Thessalonians 5:8) strengthen us against the devil's schemes.

We should examine our lives to identify areas hindering us from meeting God's standards in prayer. We must understand the truth of who we are in the Kingdom of God, stand firm in the Lord's power, and fight with the weapons He has given us. We are citizens of Heaven, ambassadors of Heaven to the earth, and ministers of reconciliation. We are children of God to whom Jesus has given authority over all the enemy's power, and we must be ready to engage the enemy and win the fight.

Chapter 3

Get Ready to Engage

Have you ever gone to the grocery store without a list and ended up buying things you didn't need? While you might remember your staple items like eggs, bread, cheese, milk, juice, and water, it's easy to forget what you already have at home or be distracted by impulse buys. The same goes for prayer—it's important to be intentional and clear about what you need, what you already have, and how to overcome the challenge you are facing. Otherwise, you may ask for unnecessary things or miss out on important aspects of your needs.

Clearly Define Your Situation

There is a clear difference between being in a fight, heading to a battle, and engaging in a war. It is important to define which one you are in because you will know what spiritual weapons are required. It is also valuable to partner with an expert in war so that you can learn from them and become one.

1. **Fight:** A *fight* is contending with and defending something or someone with force. A fight can be physical, spiritual, verbal, or psychological. When you are in a spiritual fight, it will take some force with your words, actions, and deeds to overcome your enemy.

2. **Battle:** A *battle* is an ongoing fight between two or more parties explicitly intending to win. It usually involves something of value and includes ongoing resistance. Many battles require strategic procedures that vary depending on each opponent's position.

3. **War:** A *war* is a declared battle involving a state, nation, or kingdom. It involves armed forces fighting each other on the battlefield. It involves a determined goal to occupy or defend its land, borders, its territory, and the safety of its citizens.

Hebrews 11:32-34 recounts some examples of those who fought, engaged in battle, or went to war against the enemy of God:

And what more shall I say? I do not have time to tell about Gideon, Barak, Samson, and Jephthah, about David and

Samuel and the prophets, who through faith conquered kingdoms, administered justice, and gained what was promised; who shut the mouths of lions, quenched the fury of the flames, and escaped the edge of the sword; whose weakness was turned to strength; and who became powerful in battle and routed foreign armies. (NIV)

Establishing Rules of Engagement

As the sons of God, we cannot leave the earth exposed to the enemy's agenda. God has given the believer dominion and authority to rule and reign, and it is our responsibility to respond to the things that are against the will of God. The entire earth is anxiously waiting for the Sons of God to be revealed, and Heaven has already deemed it necessary for us to deal with the atrocities happening on earth. Our mission is to establish, enforce, and carry out the will of the Father on earth. As the scriptures state in Matthew 6:10,

Thy Kingdom come, thy will be done on earth as it is in heaven. (KJV)

We have been given a charge, an assignment, an obligation, and a mission. The first of these missions is the Great Commission, and anything that contends with a believer completing this assignment is an act of war.

Everything that contends with the last instructions Jesus gave us requires a response through acts of prayer. When preparing for battle through prayer, it is vital to use foundational weapons such as acknowledging God's presence, putting on God's armor, and praying with faith and confidence.

Weapons of Warfare

Believers have access to a variety of powerful spiritual weapons for engaging in fights, battles, or wars:

- The Blood of Jesus Christ
- Unity and agreement with a believer
- Praise and worship
- Wisdom, revelation and knowledge
- The anointing of God
- Giving
- Love
- Prayer
- Repentance
- Forgiveness
- Consecration
- Fasting
- Meditating on and professing the Word of God
- Declaring the Kingdom of God Coming into the earth.

- Binding and loosing

The Foundational Weapons Are:

1. Repentance
2. Forgive, bless and release
3. Applying the blood of Jesus Christ
4. Fasting, meditation, and worship
5. Understanding God's will for the situation
6. Knowing God as Friend, Father, and Righteous Judge

When preparing to engage in a spiritual battle through prayer, you should consider that something known or unknown can delay, deter, or stop your prayers from being effective. Any legal or illegal right gained by Satan will be used against you in the battle. As a believer, you have been given spiritual weapons of mass destruction in warfare, and it is time for you to learn how to use them.

Repentance

1. Repentance requires a genuine awareness of one's wrongdoing and sinfulness.
2. It requires submitting to the lordship of Christ Jesus.
3. It involves a comprehension of God's mercy through Christ.

4. It necessitates an actual hatred of sin and a turning away from it to God.

5. It entails a persistent effort to lead a holy life by walking with God and following His commandments.

Victory in any war is achieved when the enemy surrenders or is defeated; repentance is the first sign of victory for the believer. Jesus emphasized this in Luke 5:32, stating, "I have not come to call the righteous, but sinners, to repentance." Jesus tells the Scribes and Pharisees why He came to the earth. His body and blood would pay for all of humanity's sins. He alone was chosen to make the sacrifice. No other man could do it but him because He was the son of God.

Adam and Eve, upon gaining knowledge of good and evil, failed to seek forgiveness. In contrast, however, Jesus Christ represented the second Adam, and when faced with the reality of why He came to the world, He chose obedience. In the garden of Gethsemane, He said, "Father, if you are willing, remove this cup from me," He prayed. "Nevertheless, not my will, but yours, be done" (Luke 22:42).

Jesus also had the option to choose his will and not God's—yet he chose God's. Because of this, he became the door that all humanity can come through to get back to God. The victory is in repentance and confession, causing

redemption through the blood of Christ Jesus alone as John 14:6 reads, Jesus said, "I am the way and the truth and the life. No one comes to the Father except through me." The effectiveness of your prayers depends on how quickly and honestly you respond to the things that God has sent you into the world to do. You may not have always lived according to God's will, so repentance is necessary. Your family or generations before you may not have believed in Jesus Christ, and their actions directly affect your life because of the blood you share. In all things, repentance is necessary.

To illustrate, consider military readiness. Every member of a military unit needs to pass a health screening test to ensure they are fit for duty. There may be various reasons why someone might be considered unfit or denied access to the military. Similarly, in the army of the Lord, it is crucial to understand the difference between Godly sorrow and worldly sorrow for true repentance. Godly sorrow leads to a change in behavior and actions, while worldly sorrow only causes regret and conviction without any change. Your willingness to change depends on what you value the most. If pleasing God is your top priority, you will pay close attention to what He deems valuable.

Acts 26:20 emphasizes the importance of repentance as integral to turning to God and living accordingly throughout Judea and beyond:

> *But declared first to those in Damascus and in Jerusalem, and throughout all the region of Judea, and then to the Gentiles, that they should repent, turn to God, and do works befitting repentance.*

Repentance involves a complete turnaround from sinful behaviors toward God. It requires a complete change of direction, not a partial turn. When we repent, we stop relying on our understanding of right or wrong and instead seek God's guidance. This requires placing our trust solely in God. If you feel like your thoughts, actions, or behaviors are creating a distance between you and God, it may be time to examine those areas and seek the help of the Holy Spirit to make changes.

When we repent, it's crucial to include earnest self-examination and humbly ask God for forgiveness for our sins. We should ask for the adverse effects of our sins to be removed from our lives and request that the blood of Jesus Christ be applied as payment for our sins. We must close the doors that led us to sin and ask the Holy Spirit to seal those doors. Our actions should be guided by a submission to God's authority and lordship. Take a moment to stop and pray.

Acts 5:31-32 states,

Him God has exalted to His right hand to be Prince and Savior, to give repentance to Israel and forgiveness of sins. And we are His witnesses to these things, and so also is the Holy Spirit whom God has given to those who obey Him.

Forgive, Bless, Release

Forgiveness, as highlighted in John 20:23 says,

If you forgive the sins of any, they are forgiven them; if you retain the sins of any, they are retained.

Forgiveness begins with your willingness to allow God to determine the outcome of every situation. As a matter of truth, He alone knows your beginning from your end.

Have you ever considered how holding on to unforgiveness, speaking negatively about others out loud or in your thoughts, and taking offense can harm you? These actions can allow your enemy to take control and lead your life in a negative direction. Over time, this behavior can cause you to lose ground and ultimately lose the personal battles you're fighting.

Forgiveness Is More Than Saying I'm Sorry

Forgiveness extends beyond verbal apologies; it is about finding inner peace concerning the offender's actions. It does not involve holding onto grudges or keeping a record of the wrongdoings. True forgiveness means letting go of the offense, releasing it from your soul, heart, and mind, and letting go of any associated negative emotions.

Colossians 3:12-15 encourages believers:

Therefore, as the elect of God, holy and beloved, put on tender mercies, kindness, humility, meekness, longsuffering; bearing with one another and forgiving one another, if anyone has a complaint against another; even as Christ forgave you, so you also must do. But above all these things, put on love, which is the bond of perfection. And let the peace of God rule in your hearts, to which also you were called in one body; and be thankful.

Guard Against Accusations

Forgiveness benefits both the forgiver and the forgiven. Refusing to forgive others can prevent your heavenly Father from forgiving you. Continually bringing up the wrongs others have committed against you is essentially making accusations, and the enemy (Satan) can use your words against you and those you accuse—regardless of their accuracy—to undermine you.

Matthew 6:14-15 says,

For if you forgive other people when they sin against you, your heavenly Father will also forgive you. But if you do not forgive others their sins, your Father will not forgive your sins.

The devil, also known as the accuser of the brethren, leverages unforgiveness to challenge God's plan for your life, citing sins, motives, or any unforgiveness in your heart. As per the Word of God, when you do not forgive, you are disobeying him and giving the devil an open door to accuse you of your sin before God, who is the righteous Judge.

Consider that the movement between your prayers and the answer to them is like an airplane on a runway ready for takeoff, when unforgiveness is present it causes delay and won't allow the plane to fly.

Your prayers are in a holding pattern until you address the need to forgive. Many believers feel heavy, burdened, and weighed down because they chose not to forgive. You must choose to unburden yourself and trust that God will care for you. Resolve to no longer recite the faults of others but instead fully embrace God's ability to defend you in every aspect of your life.

Invite the Holy Spirit to illuminate your heart, revealing areas where unforgiveness toward yourself or others lingers. Take time to reflect on the experiences that have burdened your mind, will, and emotions. Choose to believe in the truth of God's Word and ask for His forgiveness for your sins since you've forgiven others. You will start to experience a new sense of peace, joy, and freedom in your life.

Bless

Mathew 5:44-45 instructs,

But I say to you, love your enemies, bless those who curse you, do good to those who hate you, and pray for those who spitefully use you and persecute you, that you may be sons of your Father in heaven; for He makes His sun rise on the evil and on the good, and sends rain on the just and on the unjust.

Bless the Offender and Forgive Their Trespasses

How often do you bless the one that cursed and or mistreated you? This is not a straightforward directive to follow, but it is the will of God. It is the requirement that all believers of Christ Jesus as good soldiers in the army of the

Lord follow every example and instruction given by the Word of God. Luke 6:28 outlines the need not only to forgive but also to bless. Don't forget that when you are in battle, you must know how to use every weapon available to you.

Matthew 6:15 says,

But if you do not forgive others their sins, your Father will not forgive your sins. Bless those who curse you; pray for those who mistreat you.

Proverbs 11:25 affirms the power of blessing others:

The one who blesses others is abundantly blessed; those who help others are helped.

The most effective way to bless someone is to speak the Word of God concerning them. It is not just what you say, but it is also the intent of your heart. We were given the ability to use our mouths and words to bring life or death and to bless or curse. Desiring God's will in the life of a person who has cursed or mistreated you is a blessing. There are many occasions when the person you forgive has no idea that Satan is using them to gain an accusation against you through offense.

A sure sign that you have forgiven is being able to bless. Remember that if you forgive yourself, you should also bless yourself. If you forgive others, you should also bless them.

Release

Luke 6:36 urges:

Therefore be merciful, just as your Father also is merciful.

To release someone means to let go completely. Don't hold on to it; release it. Make space and room in your soul by releasing others from their offense. To release something is to open the door and let that thing go free. Let's consider that you or the person that you have forgiven is a prisoner of war, but you forgot or chose not to release the prisoner. Do you know a person's life may be on hold until you release them? Do you realize that your life can't progress until you release yourself? This indicates that you are fighting from a place of captivity, and the key is to forgive, bless, and release.

When Paul and Silas were imprisoned in Acts 16, they did not physically fight from a place of captivity, but they fought spiritually from a place of freedom.

They were ruling and reigning with Christ Jesus spiritually and activating the weapons of prayer and praise to respond to the battle. Paul and Silas established in the spirit the legal right to confront the works of darkness in the name of Jesus, and the judgment of God caused the prison doors to be opened.

When God passed judgment, the earth responded by shaking and opening the prison doors. The account of Paul and Silas being released miraculously from prison in Acts 16:16-40 serves as an example of how, when we respond to the challenges in life from a spiritual authority, God will intervene and turn things around in your life.

When you release the things of this world and cling to the things of God, you will begin to see results in your prayers. Release the things God does not desire for you so you can grow and achieve new heights of victory. You must release so that you can go higher and deeper in God's purpose and calling for your life.

It's time to empty those places that have held unforgiveness, offense, and the wrongdoing of self and others. It's time to see the prison doors opened and the captives set free in Jesus' Name.

1 Peter 5:6-7 says,

Therefore humble yourselves under the mighty hand of God, that He may exalt you in due time, casting all your care upon Him, for He cares for you.

Release does not mean that a person gets away with what they have done; it means you have decided to let God fight your battles like Paul and Silas did.

Applying The Blood of Jesus Christ

Preparing for spiritual battle through prayer requires understanding and applying the blood of Jesus Christ. The blood of Jesus is one of the most powerful spiritual weapons God gives us. In our physical bodies, blood is essential to life; it circulates, delivering essential substances like oxygen and nutrients while removing waste.

There is no substitute for blood; it cannot be manufactured. The blood in our body serves the purpose of transportation, regulation, and protection. Similarly, the blood of Jesus Christ accomplished our redemption through sacrifice. The blood of Jesus purifies the believer from the sin of Adam and Eve and reconnects us to God, and it keeps us alive in Christ Jesus. It also acts as our identification and protection, sealing us in God through Christ Jesus. The blood speaks about us, overcomes sin, and makes us righteous before

God. Blood becomes essential to our spiritual identity by giving us access to heavenly realms in Christ Jesus. The final blood sacrifice for all humanity was made on the cross by Jesus Christ. The first reference to shed blood in the Bible is hidden in the passage where, after man's fall, God clothed Adam and Eve with animal skins (Genesis 3:21). Blood was shed to provide Adam and Eve with a covering. In doing so, God made atonement, or a "covering," for their sin. From that time forward, God always required the shedding of innocent blood to cover man's sins. We must confess our sins, repent, ask for forgiveness, and then ask for the blood of Jesus to be applied to the sin. The shed blood of Jesus is your assurance and sign of divine protection. It may be unseen to the natural eye, but by faith, it is powerful enough to defend you from anything that Satan brings your way.

Did you know that blood has a voice? It does! After Cain slew Abel, God declared to Cain, "The voice of your brother's blood cries out to Me from the ground" (Genesis 4:10). The blood of Jesus has a voice, and Hebrews 12:24 tells us that it speaks "better things" than the blood of Abel.

The "better things" declared by Christ's blood are words of mercy, whereas Abel's blood cries for vengeance. For the believer, the shed blood of Jesus is our legal ground to have the promises in God's Word, whether it is protection, purification, or a close relationship with Him evident in our life. The blood of Jesus Christ has all power. When it spilled, it redeemed. The blood of Jesus is the life force with redemptive power to bring dead things alive.

According to Leviticus 17:11,

For the life of a creature is in the blood, and I have given it to you to make atonement for yourselves on the altar; it is the blood that makes atonement for one's life. (NIV)

Hebrews 10:4-10:

It is impossible for the blood of bulls and goats to take away sins. Therefore, when Christ came into the world, he said:

"Sacrifice and offering you did not desire, but a body you prepared for me; with burnt offerings and sin offerings you were not pleased. Then I said, 'Here I am—it is written about me in the scroll—I have come to do your will, my God.'"

First, he said, "Sacrifices and offerings, burnt offerings and sin offerings you did not desire, nor were you pleased with them"—though they were offered in accordance with the law.

Then he said, "Here I am; I have come to do your will." He
sets aside the first to establish the second. And by that will,
we have been made holy through the sacrifice of the body of
Jesus Christ once and for all.

Fasting, Meditation & Worship

Fasting is a crucial spiritual requirement that helps us prepare for prayer and spiritual battles. It's a form of worship, an offering to God, and a powerful weapon that draws us closer to Him. Fasting requires discipline, enthusiasm, and a willingness to deny ourselves so that we can seek God in spirit and truth. Through fasting, we can feed our spirit and decrease our will and desires not aligned with God's will.

Although many misunderstand fasting, it is a necessary discipline that strengthens our spirit and separates us from distractions. We must learn to embrace it to grow our relationship with God and not shy away from it.

Throughout Scripture, fasting is mentioned over 70 times, showing its significant spiritual value. The Old Testament distinguishes between two types of fasting, public and private, offering great spiritual benefits. We see Moses fasting forty days and forty nights and receiving the ten commandments from God in Exodus 34:28. It reads:

So he was there with the Lord forty days and forty nights. He neither ate bread nor drank water. And he wrote on the tablets the words of the covenant, the Ten Commandments. (Exodus 34:28 [NIV])

John 4:24 tells us,

God is Spirit, and those who worship Him must worship in spirit and truth.

To illustrate, consider military basic training or boot camp, where recruits undergo intensive physical, mental, and emotional conditioning for military service. Basic training aims to familiarize recruits with military service's physical, mental, and emotional aspects. It is an intensive process that challenges the recruits physically and psychologically to prepare them for the distinctive demands of military employment.

Similarly, fasting disciplines the spirit, strengthening and fortifying believers to grow spiritually. Spiritual strengthening, fortifying, and resilience are needed to gain power and growth in spiritual things. Fasting and praying gathers our mind, will, and emotions to the frequencies of Heaven rather than earth. Fasting reveals areas of weakness, removes barriers that stop us from hearing or seeing God, and gives us greater authority over unclean spirits.

Most importantly, fasting is a spiritual weapon used to properly transition from soul-led to spirit-led living.

The Bible provides numerous examples of individuals who fasted and received supernatural revelations and wisdom from God. Moses, Daniel, and even Jesus fasted! As per Scripture, fasting is an excellent way to develop a more intimate relationship with Christ and gain insight into what He wants to reveal.

Matthew 4:1-11 recounts the story of Jesus venturing into the wilderness where He fasted for forty days and nights. During this time, Satan tried to tempt him. The wilderness was a place of solitude where Jesus could focus on prayer without any distractions. Through fasting, Jesus found the strength to face every believer's biggest challenge: choosing God over our desires.

In response to Satan's temptations, Jesus only relied on God's written Word. The fact remains that Jesus was hungry, His body was weak, and He was separated from everything He knew, but even in the face of these challenges, He still desired the will of God. Fasting enables believers to develop the discipline to overcome spiritual and natural opposition by denying our natural wants for spiritual growth.

Meditating on the Word of God

Meditation means to think deeply or carefully about (something). Spirit-led meditation will transform and renew your mind. Reading the Bible will transform your mind, and instead of conforming to the world, it will cause you to be transformed knowing God's perfect will.

To effectively use this spiritual weapon, one must first acknowledge the value of it and understand how to wield it. The Bible is the source of divine inspiration and should be read, studied, and believed in for it to be effective. When preparing to engage in a battle through prayer, meditating on the bible is one of the most powerful spiritual weapons God gives us. The Sword of the Spirit is the Word, and by praying, reading, studying, and meditating on it, a believer sharpens their weapon and prepares themselves for spiritual warfare.

Combining the power of prayer with the biblical scripture is crucial to ensuring the effectiveness of your prayers against your enemy. Every prayer should be based on the scripture, and all strategies for establishing prayer points should be derived from it. The foundation of each targeted prayer must be the Word to respond effectively to the battle.

Holy Spirit-led meditation has an immediate positive effect on mental peace, perspective, and overall health. Moments of uncertainty or constant worrying can be silenced by meditating on scripture and spending quiet time in His presence. Meditation should always begin with meditating on Jesus Christ—who He was, who He is, and who He is to be. As Jesus Christ is the Word, meditating on the Word should begin with him and extend to God's written and spoken words.

Meditating on the bible is a spiritual weapon that is not often considered. Meditating on the Word of God equates to studying the battle plan or strategy in war. The Holy Spirit should always lead meditation. A believer's ability to focus on the Word of God, the voice of God, and the instructions of God will cause rest to their soul. It will also bring clarity and focus on the mission ahead.

Effective meditation is a weapon that combats the enemy's attack on the mind. It trains our thoughts to focus on the truth of Christ Jesus and God's intent for us. Whatever we give time and attention to will be what we believe and trust. Holy Spirit-led meditation conditions your psychological blueprint to rely on God as your source. It familiarizes you with the physical, emotional, and mental aspects of resting in God's promises.

Philippians 4:6-9 shows us how to meditate on God and His Word.

> Be anxious for nothing, but in everything by prayer and supplication, with thanksgiving, let your requests be made known to God; and the peace of God, which surpasses all understanding, will guard your hearts and minds through Christ Jesus. Finally, brethren, whatever things are true, whatever things are noble, whatever things are just, whatever things are pure, whatever things are lovely, whatever things are of good report, if there is any virtue and if there is anything praiseworthy—meditate on these things. The things which you learned and received and heard and saw in me, these do, and the God of peace will be with you. (Philippians 4:6-9)

Meditation is mentioned in the Bible in various contexts. Joshua 1:8 encourages the act of meditating on the Book of the Law day and night so that the believer can carefully follow what is written and achieve prosperity and success.

Additionally, other verses in the Bible suggest meditating on God's unfailing love (Psalm 48:9), His works and deeds (Psalm 77:12), His precepts and ways (Psalm 119:15), and His promises (Psalm 119:148).

Consider that what we meditate on is what we will eventually put into action. As believers, with the help and guidance of the Holy Spirit, we can be hearers and doers of the Word of God. The more time we spend in prayer and meditating on the Word of God, the more our strength is renewed. Psalms 119:11 says,

Thy word have I hidden in my heart so that I would not sin against you.

Worship

Worship is the heartfelt expression of our deepest affection and highest praise toward God. True worship entails loving Him with all our heart, soul, mind, and spirit, prioritizing Him first in our hearts.

Worship is a powerful spiritual weapon that draws us into His presence, where we find strength and peace. When you leave His presence, you will feel enriched and more fulfilled. Worship has the potential to cause destruction in the enemy's camp and give you victory in every battle. It also helps you focus on what is important, which is the presence of God. Worship is also an exchange where the heart and mind of God are imparted to you. In true worship, you receive strategy and a battle plan because the will of God is often revealed after being in His presence.

God is characterized as jealous, so worship, praise, honor, and adoration belong solely to Him. He will not permit anyone or anything to share in His glory. Worship is an intimate act that draws us closer to God; we know God more through worship.

Worship enables a believer to understand and comprehend God's will. Therefore, a believer must have a deep and meaningful relationship of worship with God. The revelation of God's will is only possible through the Holy Spirit, as God is a Spirit.

In John 4:21-23, Jesus speaks to the woman at the well. Jesus said to her:

> Woman, believe Me, the hour is coming when you will neither here on this mountain nor in Jerusalem, worship the Father. You worship what you do not know; we know what we worship, for salvation is of the Jews. But the hour is coming, and now is, when the true worshipers will worship the Father in spirit and truth; for the Father is seeking such to worship Him. God is Spirit, and those who worship Him must worship in spirit and truth.

Identifying the Will of God for the Situation

The fifth foundational weapon is identifying the will of God for the situation.

A critical spiritual weapon is aligning our prayers with God's will. Jesus exemplified this in Luke 22:42, surrendering His will to God in prayer. When we pray contrary to God's will, it hinders our effectiveness in spiritual warfare.

Worship exposes and counters the enemy's attacks against the believer. If you find that there are periods when you can't worship, pray, or read your Bible, it indicates that your will is under attack. The enemy can use spiritual attacks to undermine a believer's will.

When a person chooses their own will over God's will, it becomes an act of willful disobedience, which is considered a sin. It's important to acknowledge any form of disobedience and address it through repentance and by asking for the cleansing power of the blood of Jesus Christ.

A believer's will can be under attack if it is influenced by control, domination, manipulation, self-will, anti-submissiveness, or an attempt to block or hinder their will.

The believer's right and responsibility is to invite God's will into every circumstance, problem, or situation. As a believer, it's crucial to understand that the will of God is His divine plan for any situation. Since the beginning of creation, God has made provisions for all of our needs. Although we may have some insight into a problem and can see the most logical solution, it doesn't necessarily mean it aligns with God's divine plan. We may be able to see the beginning and the end of something, but the journey in between is kept from us until we can rely on His will to be done.

It's important to realize that we are never alone in our spiritual battles. Instead of following our desires, we should always seek God's will. We must allow the Holy Spirit to guide us in everything we do and surrender control to Him. If we let our minds, will, and emotions control us, we cannot follow God's will.

Romans 8:26-27 reads:

Likewise, the Spirit also helps in our weaknesses. For we do not know what we should pray for as we ought, but the Spirit Himself makes intercession for us with groanings which cannot be uttered. Now He who searches the hearts knows what the mind of the Spirit is because He makes intercession for the saints according to the will of God.

This scripture assures us that the Spirit intercedes for us according to God's will, aiding us in our weaknesses and aligning our prayers with His purposes.

Chapter 4

Using Our Five Senses to Pray

Have you ever thought about how every part of our being has a purpose? Our bodies, including their size and shape, have been the focal point of our physical development since birth. Even as babies, we are weighed and measured, a practice that continues throughout our lives.

As Christians, we understand that our identity in Christ offers a deeper perspective on why God created us. He designed our bodies to glorify Him through worship, prayer, and service. Our senses, too, are part of His intricate design and play a crucial role in our worship.

Just as God used His breath to give life to Adam, His breath lives in us, and we see how it was used in creation. All of our senses are needed to accomplish the work of God in some capacity, and they are just as important to our spiritual life as they are to our natural life.

While using all five senses is essential, the body's health, response, and positioning must be considered when engaging in a battle.

Ephesians 2:10 reads,

For we are His workmanship [His own master work, a work of art], created in Christ Jesus [reborn from above—spiritually transformed, renewed, ready to be used] for good works, which God prepared [for us] beforehand [taking paths which He set] so that we would walk in them [living the good life which He prearranged and made ready for us]. (AMP)

The 5 Senses

The five senses are vital in prayer and are utilized by the Holy Spirit to discern what is happening in a battle. In our daily lives, we rely on our senses to process information and understand various forms of communication. Likewise, believers can use their spiritual senses to gain clarity in the battle. All five senses are needed and used in the gift of discerning spirits and other things that may be unknown.

When preparing for a battle, it's essential to receive proper training and be equipped with all the necessary weapons and resources to ensure success. We cannot rely solely on our comfort zones or areas of expertise. Regarding the gifts of the Holy Spirit, it's crucial to focus on developing the gifts we are not proficient in rather than relying on our strengths. By doing so, we experience new opportunities for growth and advancement in these areas.

Eyes

The eyes serve as windows, gates, or access points to your soul. The ability to see in the spirit is a valuable aspect of prayer. We can pray effectively only when we can perceive and comprehend what the Holy Spirit communicates. It is important to note that spiritual sight and spiritual vision are different. Even though both involve the power to see, our perception often influences spiritual sight. In contrast, spiritual vision enables us to bring into focus what we see and create strategies that result in an effective outcome.

> Then the Lord answered me and said: "Write the vision and make it plain on tablets, That he may run who reads it. For the vision is yet for an appointed time; But at the end, it will speak, and it will not lie. Though it tarries, wait for it; Because it will surely come, It will not tarry."
> (Habakkuk 2:2-3)

Sometimes, during prayer, we may use our natural eyes to see, but this is unreliable as it only reflects the issues or concerns of our hearts. Since our hearts are deceitful, believers must intentionally bypass what they see in the natural world and completely connect to what the Holy Spirit shows them. It's important to note that this is the very first step in seeing.

It is crucial to remember that only some things you witness in the spiritual realm should be acted upon or discussed immediately. It is important to judge and test the visions by the Word of God and interpret all spiritual visions with the aid of scripture and guidance from the Holy Spirit. 1 Kings 18 recounts the story of the prophet Elijah, whom God sends to put an end to the drought in Israel. Elijah goes to Mt. Carmel and bows down in a position of prayer, asking God for rain. He sends his servant to look towards the sea for rain. Each time the servant returns and reports that there is no rain, Elijah sends him to look again. On the seventh time, Elijah's servant says in 1 Kings 18:44, "There is a cloud, as small as a man's hand, rising out of the sea!"

When we perceive things spiritually, it might not be apparent to us with our natural senses that the answer or promise we seek has arrived. However, the more we look and seek what the spirit reveals, the more likely we are to see it manifest in our lives.

Ephesians 1:18 says,

The eyes of your understanding being enlightened; that you may know what is the hope of His calling, what are the riches of the glory of His inheritance in the saints.

Mouth

The mouth has the power to bring life or destruction with a single breath. It's important to remember that speaking from your mind, will, or emotions won't help you win battles. However, when you speak the Word of God, you activate God's angels and strike a powerful blow against your enemy. This is because God's Word is alive, and it gives life. Just like we use our mouths to eat and taste food, we also need to use it to speak God's Word. In prayer, our sense of taste represents our appetite, and that hunger is what we bring before the Lord. That's why we should be careful with our words and discerning in all situations. The words we speak have a significant impact on our lives and those around us.

We must positively use our tongues and always speak with kindness and grace. The Bible reminds us that every word we say, good or bad, will be recorded and judged in Heaven

(Matthew 12:36). We must not let our emotions and thoughts control our speech. Instead, we should speak words of blessing, proclaim the truth of God's Word, and use our words to uplift and encourage others. We should also use our words to defend and protect humanity and to fight against the works of the enemy. One powerful declaration in prayer can crush your enemy or result in friendly fire.

Another thing we do with our mouths is to eat. Your desire must be to consume the Word of God. You will be transformed in prayer when you develop an appetite for tasting and seeing how good He is. This transformation represents growth in your prayer life, authority, and power. Psalms 34:8 says,

> *Oh, taste and see that the Lord is good! Blessed is the man*
> *who takes refuge in him!*

Hands

The hands are used to carry, transfer, or impart. It also signifies our authority. The hand of God represents His power and authority. The authority of God gives you the ability to override Satan's attempts in the life of others. We also have been given the ability to touch and feel.

The hands we use in prayer signify our agreement with Christ, the will of God, and our submission to the Holy Spirit. So, when we use the sense of touch in prayer, we seek to agree with God. We are submitting to being led and no longer leading.

The hands in agreement with God cause upward momentum and movement in the spirit. This posture allows us to move out of ourselves and elevate, ascend, modulate, or enter new places in Christ Jesus. We must go up in prayer with clean hands and a pure heart. As Psalms tells us,

Who may ascend into the hill of the Lord? Or who may stand in His holy place? He who has clean hands and a pure heart, who has not lifted up his soul to an idol, nor sworn deceitfully. (Psalms 24:3-4)

Nose

The nose is used to smell and detect, revealing what the eye cannot see. In Genesis 8:20-21, the scent of Noah's burnt offering to God caught His attention. The sense of smell deeply influences our emotions, memories, and creativity and becomes even more powerful when combined with taste. In prayer, using our sense of smell can help us identify the core issues in our soul. By doing so, we can focus our prayers on the root causes of our struggles instead of just asking for help with daily problems.

For example, there have been occasions during prayer when I have sensed the scent of a person I once knew. As I sought guidance from the Holy Spirit about this experience, I realized that I still held unresolved issues with that person and needed to forgive them. After I went through the process of forgiveness in prayer, I felt an immediate sense of relief. Following this, I started to receive answers to the situation I had been praying about.

On another occasion, I was dealing with a persistent issue and decided to fast and pray for guidance. During this time, I asked for clarity on the root cause of the problem and the people involved. One night, I had a dream in which the individuals responsible for the specific attack were revealed to me. In the dream, I also noticed two different smells, which led me to understand the presence of demonic spirits and their intentions against me. This experience involved both sight and smell, and it allowed me to uncover hidden things, which I then addressed through prayer and ultimately overcame.

Ears

The ears serve the functions of hearing and listening, with listening involving a deeper engagement than mere hearing, which is a response to sound or frequencies. This connection is crucial for spiritual, emotional, and intellectual communication. Romans. 10:17 underscores that "faith comes by hearing, and hearing by the Word of God," highlighting faith as essential for effective prayer. We must have the faith to believe that what we hear in prayer is the will of God. This only comes with knowing Him and cultivating a relationship with Him in His presence. Having an ear to hear and listen to what the Spirit is saying causes us to be precise in prayer.

It is a discipline to hear what the Spirit is saying and not listen to your soul. This comes from proper spiritual positioning, from being led by your spirit, soul, and body. Separating and identifying the truth of what we hear navigates our prayers to the precise course and goal in the battle.

Summary

Engaging all five senses is an effective weapon that can target what and how we pray. Each of our five senses has a certain percentage of effectiveness; no two functions the same way but can be used simultaneously to accomplish a specific attack. The gifts of the Holy Spirit are released to our human spirit, who relays it to our soul (mind, will, and emotion), and the body carries it out in obedience. We use our five senses to communicate the will of God and put it into action on earth.

Chapter 5

Pitfalls of Prayer

In the past, before GPS systems were available, people relied on physical maps to plan road trips. Today, GPS technology allows us to navigate to our desired destinations easily, but there are instances where it can lead us astray. In these situations, we may need to ask someone for directions. The person we ask may not provide the same kind of direction as the GPS would. They may use landmarks or points of interest instead of street names or numbers.

Similarly, prayer can be challenging for some people because there is no one right way to pray. How we communicate with God can be different from person to person, and there is no one-size-fits-all approach. Prayer can be presented in various ways, and finding a method that works best for each individual situation is essential. How do we make it make sense?

The Dos and Don'ts

1. Don't become weary

An effective weapon of spiritual warfare is endurance. You should never stop trusting, and believing God has heard you. It takes physical, mental, and spiritual strength to pray without ceasing. Be careful to avoid becoming heavy with the assignment. You must know when the assignment is over. If you remain in a battle past the time of completion, you will be exposed to weariness. Weariness can result in adverse outcomes due to a lack of clarity and strength. Galatians 6:9 says,

> Let us not become weary in doing good, for at the proper time we will reap a harvest if we do not give up.

2. Don't become routine

Praying without ceasing should not be done out of routine, but it should become a lifestyle marked by consistency. Every battle requires strategy and a plan of attack. Be intentional in your prayers and in pursuing the goal. Luke 2:36-38 describes Anna, a prophetess who served God with fasting and prayers night and day, showing dedication and purpose in her actions.

Now there was one, Anna, a prophetess, the daughter of Phanuel, of the tribe of Asher. She was of a great age and had lived with a husband seven years from her virginity, and this woman was a widow of about eighty-four years, who did not depart from the temple but served God with fasting and prayers night and day. And coming in that instant, she gave thanks to the Lord and spoke of Him to all those who looked for redemption in Jerusalem. (Luke 2:36-38)

3. Don't use your strength

Praying is an act of worship, sacrifice, surrender, submission, and warfare. Our accomplishments do not stem from our own strength; rather, it is in our weakness that His strength is perfected in us. God empowers the weak and ensures victory in our battles.

As believers, our strength lies in knowing that Jesus Christ has already secured victory in everything. Our strategy in spiritual warfare involves both offense and defense. We defend what Christ Jesus has accomplished on the earth. As sons of God, our position affirms the finality of Jesus Christ's work on the cross. It is the final say. Any deviation from the truth of who Jesus is must be brought before the Lord in prayer. This signals those who are tasked to watch and pray into active duty.

We must remember that we have agreed to be vessels for God's will to be fulfilled. Even when we witness the results of our prayers, we must acknowledge that the victory belongs to Him.

Isaiah 40:28-31 says,

Have you not known? Have you not heard? The everlasting God, the Lord, The Creator of the ends of the earth, neither faints nor is weary. His understanding is unsearchable. He gives power to the weak, and to those who have no might, He increases strength. Even the youths shall faint and be weary, And the young men shall utterly fall, but those who wait on the Lord shall renew their strength; they shall mount up with wings like eagles, they shall run and not be weary, they shall walk and not faint.

4. Don't do it alone

Praying with a partner, corporately, or as part of a group is an effective strategy to achieve your goal in prayer. Never enter the enemy's camp without direct commissioning from God, and never go alone. The power of agreement is a formidable weapon of warfare; therefore, wait for the person the Holy

Spirit leads you to and unite in agreement for the desired outcome.

No battle has ever been fought or won by one person. It takes a team of believers consistently applying their gifts to accomplish the assignment together through the power of the Holy Spirit.

Matthew 18:18-20 says,

Assuredly, I say to you, whatever you bind on earth will be bound in heaven, and whatever you loose on earth will be loosed in heaven. Again, I say to you that if two of you agree on earth concerning anything that they ask, it will be done for them by My Father in Heaven. For where two or three are gathered together in My name, I am there in the midst of them.

5. Don't pray and worry

Without faith, it is impossible to please God. Worry and anxiety diminish our faith in God's ability to answer our prayers. When we believe that God's work in our lives is complete, worry loses its foothold. Strengthen your faith by uniting with other believers. Victory is assured in every battle for those who trust in God alone.

The battle plan must be received by faith, applying it to every area of life: receiving God's promises, His Word, protection, grace, instructions, and His will. Remember, the victory has already been won.

Philippians 4:6-7 says,

Be anxious for nothing, but in everything by prayer and supplication, with thanksgiving, let your requests be made known to God; and the peace of God, which surpasses all understanding, will guard your hearts and minds through Christ Jesus.

Ephesians 6:18 advises,

With all prayer and petition pray [with specific requests] at all times [on every occasion and in every season] in the Spirit, and with this in view, stay alert with all perseverance and petition [interceding in prayer] for all God's people. (AMP)

6. Don't lose communication

Initiate daily conversations with God because battle plans can change suddenly. As a believer, you must remain flexible to God's movements and ready to respond swiftly to the Holy Spirit's promptings. When you respond this way, the result can be a cease-fire.

Invest daily time in listening to God. The sound of war can be very loud. Everything around you could be responding to the frequency of a battle. You must be prepared to discern the frequency of Heaven at all times. This requires maintaining an atmosphere of forgiveness, devoid of offense and filled with peace. Without this environment, hearing God's voice clearly and understanding His direction becomes challenging.

Jeremiah 29:12 says,

Then you will call on me and come and pray to me, and I will listen to you.

Psalm 46:10 reassures,

Be still, and know that I am God; I will be exalted among the nations, I will be exalted in the earth.

Isaiah 30:15 adds,

For thus says the Lord God, the Holy One of Israel: "In returning and rest you shall be saved; In quietness and confidence shall be your strength."

7. Be activated for every assignment

Every believer must discern if they are assigned to a specific battle. Do not assume involvement in every fight.

Sometimes, you may be called to watch, observe, and record but not engage. The Holy Spirit will prompt you when it's the battle you have been prepared for. Many soldiers remain in reserve, consistently learning and training for the moment they are called to active duty. When given an assignment, you must be activated and grow in your spiritual gifts to be effective. Each assignment will call for specific giftings to win the battle, so you must get activated.

2 Timothy 1:6 encourages,

Therefore I remind you to stir up the gift of God which is in you through the laying on of my hands.

8. Be led by the Holy Spirit

The Holy Spirit connects us with God's heart and mind. To align with His will, we must connect to the source and allow the Holy Spirit to lead us in prayer.

Living a spirit-led life enables our spirit, soul, and body to remain in continual prayer. Our human spirit and the Holy Spirit agree with God's will, which is then understood by our mind, will, and emotions and then enacted upon by our body.

Romans 8:14 declares,

For as many as are led by the Spirit of God, these are sons of God.

9. Be consistent & persistent

Be intentional and purposeful in your prayer life as a believer. Never relent in prayer, there is always a battle ongoing. We joined the spiritual fight when we received Jesus Christ as our Lord and Savior. A soldier is always a soldier, whether actively serving or not. You may be serving or a civilian, but a faithful soldier will always use the skills they've learned in training or battle to address any problem that may arise.

Establishing a routine fosters consistency in prayer. What we invest time in, tends to grow and prosper. Therefore, setting aside time to pray and seek God's guidance in addressing life's challenges is crucial. We must spend considerable time in His presence to develop a spiritual rhythm founded on intimacy with God.

It is more valuable to be recognized in the spiritual realm than to be famous in the natural world. As believers, we must prioritize what matters to God by scheduling specific times to spend with Him.

Persistence is key when seeking God, since the more we seek Him, the more we will find Him. Start with dedicating a few minutes daily to prayer at a set time and gradually increase it. This approach will help to create a spiritual appetite that will be regularly satisfied.

Colossians 4:2 advises,

Devote yourselves to prayer, being watchful and thankful.

Romans 12:12 encourages,

Be joyful in hope, patient in affliction, faithful in prayer.

10. Be submitted to the Lordship of Jesus

The driving force behind our prayers must be God's will. We must surrender our desires and align our hearts, minds, and posture in prayer to the will of God. Submission to the lordship and authority of Jesus Christ is essential.

Every soldier understands the importance of obeying their commanding officer's orders. If this is not part of your daily discipline, you aren't ready to engage in battle. Ask God to help you grow in this area before facing any conflict.

Lack of submission can lead to unnecessary casualties, which isn't God's will. Submission acknowledges God's sovereignty in all things, whether in Heaven or on the earth.

Submitting to God empowers us to resist the devil, causing him to retreat. Submitting and obeying make the battle easier to win.

Psalm 37:5 encourages,

Commit your way to the Lord, trust also in Him, and He shall bring it to pass."

James 4:7 commands,

Submit yourselves, then, to God. Resist the devil, and he will flee from you."

Chapter 6

Responding to the Battle

I have recently developed an appreciation for professional basketball. One aspect of the NBA that I particularly admire is the team's strategic response when they are in an offensive or defensive position. The team I admire has earned its reputation as one of the best in the NBA because of its exceptional defensive and offensive capabilities. When I first began watching basketball, I was drawn to a game between the two best teams. Although the team I ultimately admired the most did not win the series, their response in both the offensive and defensive positions was so impressive that I was compelled to acknowledge their resilience, diligence, and strategic assessment of the opponent's moves.

As I evaluated NBA teams, I noticed that the most successful ones excel both in offense and defense. Teams that emphasize only one aspect tend to struggle in reaching the playoffs or finals. Similarly, in prayer, it is important to respond from both an offensive and defensive position when faced with spiritual weapons of warfare. This way, we defend our position and territory on earth and actively pursue and defeat anything that seeks to contend with the will and work of our Heavenly Father. This is why we pray, "Let thy Kingdom come and let thy will be done on Earth as it is in Heaven."

Preventive War vs. Preemptive War

In the spiritual realm, we engage in two types of battles: preventive and preemptive. Preventive warfare involves strategies aimed at stopping an enemy from growing too strong to conquer in the future. If you allow your enemy to go unchecked in a situation, it can eventually overpower and rule you instead of you ruling it as God intends. Jesus Christ came and addressed Satan's unchecked activity on earth. His sacrifice on Calvary gave all human creation access to redemption from sin and access to God. We no longer had to rely on a priest to make an atonement or a sin-offering sacrifice on our behalf.

A preemptive war involves military actions aimed at preventing or defeating a potential invasion or gaining an advantage in an unavoidable conflict before the enemy strikes. This strategy ensures that the enemy is constantly under pressure and unable to gain control, keeping him under your foot.

Defensive positions refer to upholding the will of God in everyday life as a Son of God. This can be seen in a believer's response to spiritual warfare. Maintaining a continuous and effective prayer life can be compared to a military operation. It requires taking preventive and preemptive measures to prevent the enemy from attacking. In both cases, the government decides to go to war because it believes diplomatic solutions are impossible. Our government is in Christ Jesus, as mentioned in Isaiah 9:6-7,

> *For to us a child is born, to us a son is given, and the government will be on his shoulders. And He will be called Wonderful Counselor, Mighty God, Everlasting Father, Prince of Peace.*

Offense vs Defense

As human beings, you have been created in the image and likeness of God. You were given the right and the responsibility to govern the earth as God's chosen representatives. However, Adam and Eve sinned by disobeying God, and as a result, authority over the earth was lost to Satan. After Jesus' resurrection, His blood was the payment for this sin, and He was given all authority. This authority is given to you when you receive Him as your Lord and Savior. Jesus Christ said in John 14:6,

> I am the way, the truth, and the life; no one can come to the Father except through me. (NIV)

The believer's assignment as soldiers in the army of the Lord, sons of God and His redeemed in the earth, is to enforce the finished work of Jesus Christ. God's will, which is His divine order, must be maintained on earth. This truth puts the believer in direct war with the enemy.

As believers, it is essential to seek the Lord for guidance before assuming what is needed in every battle. You should not think you are meant to figure out the strategy alone. A pitfall in responding to the war is not getting the specific battle plans from God. It is like running into a fire without protection. The result will always be a loss, so you must never face a challenge based on your emotions. You should always stop, seek God in prayer for revelation, and then respond based on the instructions given to you by the Holy Spirit. You are instructed to follow Jesus' example by asking God for help and strength when facing life's challenges.

The Holy Spirit is your help. He is the Spirit of God and the Spirit of Truth. To the believer, the Holy Spirit is a gift and treasure that gives you an advantage in the battles you are fighting. The Holy Spirit reveals the mysteries of the Gospel and uncovers hidden things. When you face a struggle, you must pray for the Spirit of Wisdom, Knowledge, Might, Understanding, the Fear of the Lord, and Counsel. These can only be received by the Holy Spirit and are the weapons that help you triumph in the face of adversity.

Offense

In spiritual warfare, prayer is the believer's response. I would like you to consider two prayer positions: offensive and defensive. While the offensive position is favorable, it is chosen based on a response to a targeted spiritual attack. When taking the offensive approach, a believer's response is purely motivated by the fact that a specific issue has arisen and requires you to defend it.

Responding offensively is reactive, while responding defensively is proactive. One challenge of reacting solely when under attack is that it creates a cycle and belief that you don't always have an adversary; you begin to believe that you only have to fight at specific times and for particular occurrences, and your adversary won't return. This is a lie and a misrepresentation of who you are in Christ Jesus and your identity. This mindset can lead to complacency, causing you to overlook potential threats. It is important to stay alert and pray always. Jesus said in John 10:10,

> The thief does not come except to steal, and to kill, and to destroy. I have come that they may have life and that they may have it more abundantly.

1 Peter 5:8 tells us,

> Be sober, be vigilant; because your adversary the devil walks about like a roaring lion, seeking whom he may devour.

As a believer, you must be aware that the devil is your adversary, and he desires to take as many people to hell with him as possible. It's important to note that God did not create hell for humanity but as the place of judgment for the fallen angels. Therefore, your response should not be limited to fighting your personal battles in prayer only, but also applied to those whom God has given you influence.

Approaching prayer as an offensive spiritual tactic may yield short-term benefits. One potential disadvantage of this position is that your initial reaction to a spiritual attack may be driven by emotions rather than guided by the Holy Spirit. This can lead you to deviate from God's plan, unknowingly or knowingly. As believers, our call is to align ourselves with God's will, as Jesus Christ did when He came to dismantle the works of the enemy.

Let's consider the responsibilities of a police officer. First, a person must decide that they are willing to uphold, abide by, and submit to the authority and laws of the land. They must learn the laws that have been enacted and put in place before becoming a police officer and be willing to submit themselves to the authority of that government.

Moreover, they must be willing to make the ultimate sacrifice to defend and protect the lives of others. A police officer's primary duty is to uphold and enforce the law. The most effective way to enforce the law is by monitoring, protecting, and being accountable for it. Similarly, the best way to uphold the finished work of Christ Jesus in the world requires a believer to maintain spiritual readiness and never lose sight of what is truly important to God.

You must prioritize obeying God and building a solid relationship through prayer. Your focus and motivation should be to obey what was revealed in prayer. Don't wait for the enemy to attack you to use the weapons God has given you;

instead, readily enforce, steward, and govern what Jesus Christ has done.

When taking an offensive position, remember to:

- Be free from all sin and repent for any broken covenant to God.
- Forgive, bless, and release all offenses.
- Seek God's mind, heart, and desire before responding.
- Examine your thoughts and maintain a desire to please God.
- Allow God to take control. Do not fight His will; know His will and obey.
- Don't force or pray your will on anyone else.
- Obtain the biblical strategy and prayer points for your response.
- Remain consistent and persistent without losing hope or faith in God's Word.
- Then rest.

Defense

The believer's defensive position is always to be prepared to defend and enforce God's will and the victory that has been won. To defend means to protect someone or something from harm or danger by resisting an attack. A believer's defensive response during a war is intended to uphold Jesus Christ's victory on the cross.

Exodus 15:2-3 says,

The LORD is my strength and my defense; he has become my salvation. He is my God, and I will praise him, my father's God, and I will exalt him. The LORD is a warrior; the LORD is his name.

A believer is called to pray in obedience to maintain the order and will of God in the world. A believer's defensive response is demonstrated by occupying until Jesus returns, thereby applying the spiritual weapons obtained by the Holy Spirit to free those in bondage.

For example, when two countries go to war and victory is declared, securing and occupying the territory and land is important. A gate and defense perimeter must be set up to prevent further attacks, ensuring that the enemy can't sneak in and regain control. A new governmental system is established, and soldiers are stationed to watch, survey, oversee, and defend the ground already won.

Preventative measures must be put in place in the spirit and naturally to ensure that when the enemy comes back around to attack, you are ready for him. As believers, when you pray in a defensive posture, you must remember that your goal is to pray for God's will. Each person plays a role in God's design, which is that no one is lost and that all come to know the gift He has given us, which is salvation through Jesus Christ.

The threat of the adversary is always present, and your response should be to continually destroy the works of the enemy by standing your ground in truth, speaking, and declaring God's governmental system on earth. This means disagreeing with everything that goes against Jesus and your identity in Christ Jesus.

When you clearly understand what you are defending, it becomes easier to comprehend the frequency of prayer necessary to uphold your position of authority and power. This position represents a defensive response instead of an offensive response.

After successfully overcoming the adversary's attack, it is important to remain vigilant and pray. You must take control of the territory, gates, and doors you gained authority over. One way to achieve this is by being intentional about your thoughts, actions, words, and deeds and managing your time wisely. As you have the experience of winning a battle, you can use your knowledge to help someone facing a similar situation. You can now share your battle strategies and tactics with others. Additionally, it would be best to consider utilizing the wisdom and knowledge gained during the battle, as they hold tremendous value in the spiritual realm. The victory that comes with answered prayers could manifest as a child's healing or a spouse's salvation.

Your main objective is to assist those unaware of the truth of the gospel of Jesus Christ.

> But even if our gospel is veiled, it is veiled to those who are perishing, whose minds the god of this age has blinded, who do not believe, lest the light of the gospel of the glory of Christ, who is the image of God, should shine on them. (2 Corinthians 4:3-4)

A defensive response in prayer can be seen in how you distribute your time, discipline your life, and submit and obey the Lordship of Christ. It looks like a life submitted to being set apart for the use of God with one focus and purpose.

When you pray defensively, you produce precision and correctly identify the underlying problems by exposing the tactics and strategies of the enemy, allowing God's light to shine through. A defensive response in prayer requires a clear understanding that although you are in this world, you are not of this world. All the works of man's hands will be judged. A defensive response is always motivated by the spirit and not the soul. Your response should be driven by your desire to store treasures in Heaven for your eternal life, not your temporary life here on Earth.

A defensive response does not sit back and wait until the enemy launches an attack but preemptively strikes blows to the enemy's agenda in the spirit. The adversary is always conspiring to kill, steal, and destroy, and because we know this truth, a position of defense is required to be fully effective in the war of the Kingdom of God. The enemy attacks naturally and spiritually in three ways: to kill, steal, and destroy. This can happen not only in the physical realm but also in the spiritual, emotional, and mental realms. The goal is not only to harm you but also to impact your bloodline for generations to come. This effect can last long after you have passed away. With this truth, you can defensively counteract the enemy's intent in prayer, which has a long-lasting impact by releasing the Word and promises of God to you and your future generations.

When in a position of defense, remember to spiritually:

- Secure your borders, paths, bridges, gates, doors, and airways.
- Re-align your battle strategy and shift positions as the Holy Spirit leads.
- Do not be caught unaware or unprepared.
- Check the seed of the heart, ensuring it is pleasing to God.

For the greatest results in prayer, a believer should consider combining the offensive and defensive positions.

When you sense that something in your life is out of order or leading you away from God, it indicates an attack against you.

You should respond by not ignoring or dismissing what you see or feel. It's crucial to respond by seeking God more frequently. Set specific times for prayer and fasting to maintain submission of your soul and body to the Lordship of Christ. It is also crucial to make necessary pivots and adjustments and regularly review your defensive strategy to address the adversary as a defender. Another effective defensive response in a spiritual battle is applying the principle of resting and resolving in the truth that God hears your prayers. By implementing both strategies against the enemy, he will not gain the upper hand against you.

Your Window of Opportunity

When initiating a preemptive strike, you must be sensitive and discerning when a window of opportunity is available in the spirit.

A window of opportunity opens when there is a perceived or actual shift in the balance of power that favors the believer. Sometimes, a window of opportunity is sensed in prayer but not seen. Sometimes, it may be known in prayer but must be fully understood. It may also feel or look like a flow, sequence, or constant revealing of something specific.

As a believer, when such a window of opportunity presents itself, you can seize it to gain spiritual ground and territory, leading to visible transformation in your life.

This can be achieved by joining a large gathering or corporate body of equipped, empowered believers with the same assignment. They can be considered a military-ranked brigade or regiment. In this environment, unity in the spirit has already been established, and you use the opportunity to address the battle you are fighting with the backing of many believers in the spirit and the natural.

Windows of opportunity often involve angelic assistance. Psalm 91:11 assures us that God commands His angels to guard us in all our ways. Asking God to send His angels to fight on our behalf is a crucial strategy in spiritual warfare, as illustrated in Daniel 10:10-21. When Daniel prayed sincerely, God sent an angel to bring him an answer and a message.

Ephesians 6:12 reminds us that we wrestle not against flesh and blood but against principalities, powers, rulers of the darkness of this world, and spiritual wickedness in high places. In such a context, a window of opportunity is a specific period when the enemy has retreated, and you are empowered to move forward in the ground you have gained by the power of the Holy Spirit. In these instances, you can take a breath or pursue further and gain additional ground.

Windows of opportunities are appointed or released at specific times:

There are instances in the Bible when Jesus would respond to situations and problems based on whether it was the appointed time to address them. He knew the day and the hour for the work He was sent to accomplish. He consistently communicated to those close to Him not to make Him step out of the Father's time into theirs because of a need.

In John 17:1, Jesus acknowledged His appointed time by lifting His eyes to Heaven and saying,

Father, the hour has come. Glorify Your Son, that Your Son also may glorify You, as You have given Him authority over all flesh, that He should give eternal life to as many as You have given Him. And this is eternal life, that they may know You, the only true God, and Jesus Christ whom You have sent. I have glorified You on the earth. I have finished the work which You have given Me to do. And now, O Father, glorify Me together with Yourself, with the glory which I had with You before the world was.

When a window of opportunity comes, it is important to:

- Recognize it and respond to it correctly by deciding if you will pursue it or rest.
- Expect a favorable result using proven spiritual weapons.
- Move in time, with momentum, and by the speed of the holy spirit.

When you identify a window of opportunity has opened to you, respond in prayer by establishing the *divine protection* of God as noted in Psalm 91:1-2. Preemptively declare the *time of warfare* according to Psalm 144: 1-2.

A believer's response to war rests in the truth that God gives us divine protection. Whether responding to a battle or pursuing an enemy, we need divine angelic assistance. Request from God *divine angelic assistance* on your behalf, as seen in Daniel 10:13. Expect *heightened angelic activity* in the spiritual realm on your behalf, as noted in Joshua 5:13. Maximize the set times you watch and pray; refer to Matthew 24:42-44.

A believer's response to war in prayer will also look like a period of rest.

There are some battles you don't need to fight to win; instead, you rest in your sonship. This is called governing from a seat of rest.

Rest is confidence in God's perfected work being finished in our lives.

> *Come to Me, all you who are weary and burdened, and I will give you rest. Take My yoke upon you and learn from Me, for I am gentle and lowly in heart, and you will find rest for your souls. For My yoke is easy, and My burden is light. (Matthew 11:28-30)*

When a believer responds to spiritual war from a place of rest, it does not mean that we stop acting, but it means that we strategically enter a period where we rely on God's response. The response of rest can be instituted by the following types:

1. Physical Rest
2. Mental Rest
3. Social Rest
4. Spiritual Rest
5. Visual, Audio, Verbal Rest
6. Emotional Rest
7. Creative Rest

God's Rest gives us His direct response to conflict, causing us to win the war by turning the tide.

Chapter 7

Defending the Kingdom of God on Earth

When I think about the idea of a kingdom, my mind naturally goes to my mother. She was born in the United Kingdom and her childhood stories helped me form a connection with a monarchy, despite growing up in a democratic environment in the United States. As I became an adult and traveled to the UK, I gained a deeper appreciation for her perspective. Living in a kingdom profoundly influenced my mother's identity, which was evident in how she nurtured and guided my siblings and me.

When we believe in Jesus Christ, we are welcomed into God's Kingdom. Even if we think we know what it means to be part of it, we can fully understand who we are only when we submit to His lordship. We can choose to be passive spectators of the Kingdom of God, or we can choose to take full residency in it, accessing everything that has been given to us through the redemption of Jesus Christ. We are gifted with citizenship in both Heaven and Earth. In the natural sense, this would be like having dual citizenship, similar to what I could request from the United Kingdom because my mother was born there. Belonging to the Kingdom of God offers us the privilege of having the power and authority of God, which works on our behalf both in the spiritual and physical realms. As believers, we are granted access to God's sovereignty and dominion in the heavens and earth.

This is a valuable inheritance that must be defended. Matthew 11:12 says,

> And from the days of John the Baptist until now the kingdom of heaven suffers violence, and the violent take it by force.

In John 18:36, Jesus answers Pilate's question about whether He is the King of the Jews by stating,

> My kingdom is not of this world. If it were, my servants would fight to prevent my arrest by the Jewish leaders. But now my kingdom is from another place. (NIV)

As a believer, you belong to the Kingdom of God. There are two kingdoms—one of light and one of darkness. The kingdom of darkness is constantly at odds with the Kingdom of Light. As a Christian, you have chosen to follow Jesus, who is the light of the world, and therefore, you belong to the Kingdom of God. The kingdom of Darkness wars against what you believe, your identity, and the gift of eternal life given to you.

The Kingdom of God restores your true identity and makes you who God designed you to be. Realizing your true identity transforms your imagination and gives you a clear vision of your purpose on earth.

Revelation 11:15 says,

The seventh angel sounded his trumpet, and there were loud voices in heaven, which said: "The kingdom of the world has become the kingdom of our Lord and of his Messiah, and he will reign forever and ever." (NIV)

The Kingdom of God is the government established in Heaven and on Earth. When Jesus Christ came, he brought the Kingdom of God. Jesus came with the power and authority of the Kingdom of God and revealed it to humanity.

In the Kingdom of God, a believer's response to the war in prayer involves identifying their assignment and rescuing lost souls. Prayer is used carefully, accurately, and diligently to seek these revelations.

When entering the Kingdom of God, it's important to understand that our weapons of warfare are not physical but spiritual, powerful, and effective. As believers, we trade our natural weapons for supernatural ones. Jesus instructed His disciples to wait for the Holy Spirit, and when He came in Acts 2:4, they received power and authority.

It's vital to have a flexible and discerning approach to understanding how battles are fought in the spiritual realm compared to how we fight in the physical world. As believers, the same Holy Spirit that raised Jesus Christ from the dead lives within us, and we cannot use worldly weapons to overcome spiritual attacks.

When responding to war in prayer, it's important to remember that God's anointing alone is not enough. Your effectiveness in the spiritual realm will depend on how you use the anointing of God, power, and authority in the name of Jesus Christ. Having authority in the name of Jesus gives you the right to declare, exercise, and enforce His will. Jesus Christ has given us the authority to override any prevailing negative judgment through prayer. We can approach Him in the heavens, as we are now seated in heavenly places in Christ Jesus, according to Ephesians 2:6.

The Kingdom of God acknowledges when it is time for warfare. God's authority is meant for warfare, and the Holy Spirit empowers you to change, shift, and move situations in your life and the lives of others. You have been granted the authority to reject what is not in line with God's will for you and ask for His desires to be established on Earth as they are in Heaven. As a believer, it is important to ensure that your desires do not conflict with God's desires. When responding to war as a believer, you understand that the power given to you is from the Lord, and you are, therefore, submitted to His will.

It is more significant to be great in the Kingdom of God than in the kingdom of man.

> But seek first his kingdom and his righteousness, and all these things will be given to you as well. Therefore, do not worry about tomorrow, for tomorrow will worry about itself. Each day has enough trouble of its own. (Matthew 6:33-34.

The power of prayer holds profound significance and purpose. However, the only thing that can stop God's power from working in your life is your decision not to obey Him. The kingdom of darkness has set up various systems in this world to keep you away from God and His plan for your life. The weapon you can use to overcome these attacks is determination. When you have determination, you develop staying power, enabling you to be resilient in life's challenges. When a believer responds with determination in prayer, they rely on the spiritual truth found in 1 John 4:4. As a believer, you must take care not to fall prey to having a form of godliness because of the spirit of error. Daily examination of your motives and agendas is required in prayer before engaging in any warfare.

> *You are of God, little children, and have overcome them, because He who is in you is greater than he who is in the world. 5 They are of the world. Therefore, they speak as of the world, and the world hears them. 6 We are of God. He who knows God hears us; he who is not of God does not hear us. By this, we know the spirit of truth and the spirit of error. (1 John 4:4-6)*

As a believer, responding to spiritual warfare in prayer is important because a divided kingdom cannot stand. God has chosen you to use the power and authority given by the Holy Spirit to establish His governmental authority on earth.

During prayer, you can stand on what you see, hear, and what is revealed to you by the Holy Spirit's leading. We see the Kingdom of God established when we speak to a situation as sons of God, and it becomes tangible in life.

A believer's response to war in prayer is a daily lifestyle that must be cultivated to grow. Your ability to maximize what is available in the Kingdom of God begins with your willingness to prioritize what is important to God first. If you apply these spiritual weapons of warfare in prayer, God's will can be established in your life. Let everyone be subject to God's governing authorities, for there is no authority except that which God has established.

Chapter 8

Righteous Judgment

God established His authority in Heaven and on Earth. As His delegated authority and appointed representatives here, it is crucial that we seek God's judgment to be executed in spiritual matters. When spiritual forces oppose us, asking for God's judgment from Heaven into Earth is essential.

Various spiritual forces in our surroundings launch attacks against our lives. The most common attack used by our enemy is accusations. The warfare tactic of accusations is not new. It has existed from the beginning. In Genesis 3:11-13, Adam accuses Eve of leading him to disobey God's instructions, and Eve blames the serpent for influencing her disobedience and Adam's decision. As a result, God pronounces judgment on Adam, Eve, their descendants, and the serpent. This is why every person is born into sin and shaped by iniquity. Iniquity is essentially a generational curse of the bloodline; The atonement achieved through the shedding of Jesus Christ's blood absolves believers from this judgment. During challenging times, it is vital to recall that God's authority transcends all.

> *Then I heard a loud voice in heaven say: "Now have come the salvation and the power and the kingdom of our God, and the authority of his Messiah. For the accuser of our brothers and sisters, who accuses them before our God day and night, has been hurled down. They triumphed over him by the blood of the Lamb and by the word of their testimony; they did not love their lives so much as to shrink from death."*

> *Therefore rejoice, you heavens and you who dwell in them! But woe to the earth and the sea because the devil has gone down to you! He is filled with fury because he knows that his time is short. (Revelation 12:10-12)*

As believers, we are inclined to battle with our emotions and our natural strength, but we must utilize the ability to take our concerns to the righteous Judge in the courts of the Lord. It is beneficial to seek His righteous judgment when faced with accusations and attacks. I have consistently experienced a tremendous outcome to stubborn problems and delayed prayer responses when I approach God as my righteous Judge in the court of the Lord.

Who is a God like you, who pardons sin and forgives the transgression of the remnant of his inheritance? You do not stay angry forever but delight in showing mercy. You will again have compassion on us; you will tread our sins underfoot and hurl all our iniquities into the depths of the sea. (Micah 7:18-19)

Praying to God in his role as the righteous Judge occurs in His Court of Mercy. We agree with the adversary's accusation (Matthew 5:25-26), we confess the accusation as sin (1 John 1:9), we repent of the sin (Proverbs 28:13), we forgive, bless, and release ourselves and anyone that introduces that sin into our lives, we ask that the blood of Jesus Christ be applied to that sin (1 John 1:7). We then request the judgment of the righteous Judge and wait for the Holy Spirit to give us the peace that this prayer has been heard and receive His judgment into our hearts. After receiving the Lord's judgment, we should ask that He send His angels to assist in establishing His will in our lives.

For he will command his angels concerning you to guard you in all your ways. (Psalm 91:11 [NIV])

Chapter 9

Heavenly Enforcement Agents

For he will command his angels concerning you to guard
you in all your ways. (Psalms 91:11 [NIV])

In spiritual battles, asking God for help is crucial. According to Psalms 91:11, God commands His angels to protect us in all our ways during these battles. It's important to be properly guarded in the spirit. The angels of the Lord surround those who fear the Lord, and we are constantly being guarded and protected by them. Some battles require increased angelic assistance. In addition to the help from the angels, the Holy Spirit is our comforter, instructor, and defender, while Jesus Christ is our great advocate, making intercession on our behalf.

God created angels to serve a purpose, including warfare angels that fight battles in the unseen realm. Therefore, asking God to dispatch His angels to guard and protect us when we need their assistance is very important. It is important to note that we do not worship angels, but God has given us spiritual backup by His angelic army. They await the prayers of the righteous so that they can actively engage in assisting in establishing the promises of God in our lives.

Angels and the assistance of angels have been mentioned throughout the Bible.

Psalms 8:2-6 really puts into perspective the intent of God for man. It says,

You have set your glory in the heavens. Through the praise of children and infants, you have established a stronghold against your enemies to silence the foe and the avenger.

When I consider your heavens, the work of your fingers, the moon and the stars, which you have set in place, what is humankind that you are mindful of them, human beings that you care for them? You have made them a little lower than the angels and crowned them with glory and honor. You made them rulers over the works of your hands; you put everything under their feet. (NIV)

In everything God created us to do, He intended for us to rule, and the angels of the Lord assist us in accomplishing that work. Scripture provides numerous accounts of angels communicating with or aiding in God's work, such as in Matthew 1:20, 1:24, 2:13, 2:19, 28:2; Luke 1:11, 2:9; John 5:4; Acts 5:19, 8:26, 12:7, and 12:23.

Chapter 10

Breaking Through

As believers, we engage in battle because we recognize that strategies and structures exist to keep us in bondage, hold us back, and prevent us from succeeding in God's purpose and plan for our lives.

You may look back on your life and realize there has been a persistent issue you have been unable to overcome. For me, I struggled to maintain a pregnancy. I experienced several pregnancy losses beginning at the age of sixteen years old, and each time, I trusted, hoped, and believed it would result in a child. Unfortunately, I suffered six losses before finally having a child at the age of thirty-seven. Throughout my journey to become a mother, I faced repeated heartbreak, never truly understanding why the outcome differed from what I believed God had promised me. This, indeed, was a stubborn situation, to put it kindly. One day, I stopped trying and believing, and I stopped expecting to be a mother. For over a year, whenever someone asked if we were trying to conceive, my husband and I would respond, "No, we are not trying again." But one day, I was driving, and the Holy Spirit asked me a question: He asked me if I genuinely believed that the promise of God was true. I immediately responded yes; I believed it was true, and I knew then that I had to keep fighting until I saw the promise of God to have a child materialize in my life. It took two more attempts before I held my son in my arms. Many acts of faith, war, and prayer overcame this stubborn situation.

When I realized I believed in God's Word more than anything else, I was determined to do whatever was required. I may have given up on God and His promise, but He did not give up on me or His Word. He honored and fulfilled His Word in His time. The difference between a believer and a nonbeliever in any battle, especially a difficult one, is that a believer always returns to what initially motivated them to engage in the fight.

When facing a stubborn battle, you must regroup and ask yourself some questions. What motivated you to believe in the first place? What determination do you have, and how much more do you need to endure to the end? Some battles and stubborn situations result from previous generations that have come before you. Still, regardless of how the war began, God intends to give you victory as long as you endure. A key weapon is to ask God for His enduring grace to overcome the stubborn situation.

Strategies for Stubborn Situations

Begin by taking stock of what you already know about the situation. It's vital to assess the knowledge, strategies, tactics, life experiences, spiritual insights, teachings, manifestations, revelations, and truths you have accumulated over the years. All of these are considered weapons that you have stored within you, and the challenging situation may require you to use everything you know or even something greater that you have yet to discover, perhaps from someone who has successfully overcome a similar challenge.

There are often hidden truths and spiritual legalities used against you and other members of your bloodline in past generations. If the Holy Spirit reveals these truths, they could explain why a stubborn situation has resisted your efforts to overcome it.

Dealing with a stubborn situation requires spiritual resilience, determination, tenacity, endurance, strength, and the full support of Heaven. It's also crucial to completely align with God's will concerning the situation. Any deviation from

God's will in addressing a stubborn situation will prevent it from changing.

In a challenging situation, the key to making a difference also lies in the support of those God sends your way to aid you in your situation. They will have profound knowledge and expertise in the situation you are facing and can help you make sense of things. They are often called destiny helpers.

It will also require the assistance of fellow believers to intercede and stand in the gap on your behalf. Overcoming the challenge will demand multiple efforts against the adversary and the collaboration of many individuals aligned with the will of God. It could systematically happen in a moment, but it could also occur over time. Many people give up and surrender in the middle of a battle because they are weary. You won't see the fullness of the promise of God if you don't endure to the end.

The Steps Needed

First, we need to identify any commonalities, similarities, or patterns. We should look for previous occurrences of this stubborn situation in the family or the person's life and determine where it manifests itself. Once we have identified the commonality or similarity, the next step is to identify the legal rights, authorities, agreements, or covenants that allow this stubborn situation to persist. Once identified, deep repentance is needed on multiple levels. Deep repentance may be necessary on your behalf, on behalf of your generations, on behalf of your spouse, and even on behalf of your community. Always be willing to repent and ask for forgiveness. It is a gift from God.

Never forget that God is always working things out for your good. Jesus Christ is advocating on your behalf in the forefront, so you never have to question if you are in the fight alone.

Deuteronomy 1:30 says,

The Lord your God who goes before you will himself fight
for you, just as he did for you in Egypt before your eyes.

However, you do have to be very precise as to what is working behind the scenes and how it is being backed in the spirit. Every demonic assignment, spiritual battle, and war receives support from a higher authority, whether a person, place, or thing. Therefore, don't view a stubborn situation as a random occurrence. Every stubborn situation has the support of good or evil. You must identify these initial forces to gain the upper hand when applying the Word of God to overcome the situation. Evaluate who benefits from the situation. Will it bring glory to God or cause you to turn away? You must understand the end goal of the situation to remove it.

What I had to overcome in my situation was not only reaching a point of enduring, believing, hoping, and trusting in God again but also repenting for expressing that I no longer wanted to have a child and that I no longer wanted to try. I had to break the covenant and agreement with the words I spoke because they were not aligned with God's will. My spoken words also caused delays. Subsequently, beginning in my childhood and through my adulthood, some things were spoken over me or done to me that contributed to the stubborn situation. There were also works of someone's hands or acts of those who came before me in my generation that significantly impacted my ability to produce the fruit of the womb. But most of all, the value of my child's life in the Kingdom of God is great. My strategy to overcome also took a team of six doctors, who partnered with the promise of God; they joined their faith with my faith and took extraordinary measures to do their part. I also encountered many believers willing to fight, pray, and speak the Word of God over my stubborn situation, each one being a destiny helper.

Strategic Prayers

And it shall come to pass in the last days, says God, that I will pour out of my spirit on all flesh. (Acts 2:17)

We are currently witnessing a time of great turmoil and conflict. Wars and rumors of wars are rampant, and evil forces seem to be gaining ground on Earth. Notably, persecution of believers is on the rise. However, as we navigate this challenging period, we must remember that God has granted us the power and authority to defeat the enemy's works. We use our weapons of prayer to bring God's will into the earth.

Chapter 11

Guided Prayer Examples

Feel free to use these prayer examples as a guide for your prayers:

Purification and Preparation

Repentance Prayer Example

Repentance is a powerful weapon against the enemy's accusations. This act places your sins under the blood of Jesus and removes the enemy's ability to accuse you.

I agree with the adversary according to Matthew 5:25-26. Yes, I committed these sins knowing or unknowingly, willingly or unwillingly. I confess my sins and transgressions according to 1 John 1:9, and I repent of these sins according to Proverbs 28:13. I ask for Your forgiveness and for the blood of Jesus Christ to be applied to my life (as stated in 1 John 1:7) and recorded in my book in Heaven.

*I **repent** for all willful disobedience and for allowing my mind, will, and emotions to dictate my actions. I ask you, God, to forgive me and apply the blood of Jesus Christ to this sin.*

*I **repent** for agreeing with the things that were not your will and ask you, God, to forgive me and apply the blood of Jesus Christ to this sin. I come out of agreement with the works of the flesh; the desires of my mind, will, and emotions will no longer lead me from this day forward. I choose to be led by the Spirit of God, as those whom the Spirit of God leads are the Sons of God. I ask you to forgive me and apply the blood of Jesus Christ to this sin.*

*I **repent** and lay aside every weight and every sin that so quickly ensnared me, and I choose to get back in the race set before me as I look unto Jesus, the author and finisher of my faith. I ask you to forgive me and apply the blood of Jesus Christ to this sin.*

*I **repent** for agreeing with disobedience, willful disobedience, rebellion, and dishonor. I ask you to forgive me of this transgression and ask that the blood of Jesus Christ be applied to this sin and everything it produced. I ask you, Holy Spirit, to examine my heart today, my motives, my intent, and my agenda.*

*I **repent** for all areas not in your will and ask for your forgiveness.*

I renounce every demonic agreement, covenant, oath, barter, and vow made knowingly or unknowingly by me or by someone in my family. I ask you, Father, righteous Judge, and friend, to forgive us and apply the blood of Jesus Christ to this sin.

I **repent** for broken covenants, broken promises, broken vows, and broken agreements to you, and I ask your forgiveness now and that the blood of Jesus Christ be applied to this sin.

I **repent** for using my mouth to speak against your work, your people, myself, or my family. May my negative words that bring death be canceled and your words that bring life be restored. I ask you to forgive me of this sin and apply the blood of Jesus Christ to it.

I **repent** for not working during the day, putting my hand to the plow in the earth, and not fully committing to your assignment or instructions. **I repent for allowing my desires to interfere with your assignment.** I ask you to forgive me and apply the blood of Jesus Christ to this sin. I asked that everything that was birthed due to this sin come to an end in Jesus' name.

I **repent** for opening the door to the devil through sin, transgressions, iniquities, and unforgiveness. I choose to close that door through repentance. I call my actions, thoughts, and behavior sin, and I ask your forgiveness now in Jesus' name. I ask that the blood of Jesus be the payment for this sin. I am confessing my sins, as you oh God are faithful and just to forgive me and clean me from all unrighteousness. I ask you to apply the blood of Jesus Christ to this sin. I ask that as far as the East is from the West, you forgive all my transgressions, sins, and iniquities in Jesus' name, amen.

Engaging in the Battle for Freedom

Use this prayer as a guide for gaining freedom in any situation:

Example Prayer

In 2 Corinthians 3:17, it says, 'Now the Lord is the Spirit, and where the Spirit of the Lord is, there is freedom.' Similarly, 1 Corinthians 2:12 states, 'Now we have received, not the spirit of the world, but the Spirit who is from God, that we might know the things that have been freely given to us by God.'

According to these scriptures, Heavenly Father, I thank You for our liberty and freedom in Christ Jesus. I will stand firmly in the liberty by which Christ has made us accessible. I will not be entangled again with any yoke of bondage. Thank you, Lord, for calling me to liberty and freedom. I declare that I will not use this freedom to sin against you, but I will use it to serve others in Christ's love.

I praise You for breaking the bonds and chains of captivity, and we now war from a place of freedom. I confess and believe I have freedom in my mind, thoughts, imaginations, perceptions, and views. I will look not only to my interests but also to the interests of others. I will have the same mindset of Christ Jesus. I am determined to walk in freedom by working out my soul salvation with fear and trembling in Jesus' name.

I declare freedom in my family; every chain and place of captivity that operated in the minds of my family is being broken and destroyed in the name of Jesus Christ.

I decree freedom in my marriage and relationships in the name of Jesus Christ and break the power and influence of the spirit of division and discord in the name of Jesus.

I decree freedom in my finances in the name of Jesus, for you give seed to the sower. Make me a lender and not a borrower, heavenly Father. Give me access to my harvest and the seeds sown in seasons past in Jesus' name, for you are Lord of the harvest.

Make my finances expand and grow. Change it to the currency of Heaven, causing it to multiply and increase in Jesus' name. Expand and elevate my economic position and increase my assets in Jesus' name.

I decree freedom and healing in our mental health, emotions, and memories. I will speak life over challenges and every lie of the devil. I decree and declare we will be stable in all our ways in the name of Jesus Christ. My mind will be stable, and I will win every battle against my mind in the name of Jesus!

Every time the enemy comes in like a flood, the Spirit of the Lord will lift up a standard against it. May that stand prompt angelic assistants to shut the mouths of the enemy who projects thoughts that come to destroy us in the name of Jesus Christ. I decree freedom in my walk with Christ, my commitment to God and the ministry, and the working of the Holy Spirit in my life and the lives of others. I will occupy and possess the things of God and not my wants and desires.

I declare freedom in my will, emotions, and mind in Jesus' name. My soul will be free in Jesus' name. I will occupy and possess freedom, committing my ways to God, and He will give me the desire of our hearts. I will be free in ministry, for I know that the harvest is plenty, but the laborers are few.

I decree that Freedom in every aspect of my life will be my portion in Jesus' name. Amen.

Engaging Your Five Senses in Battle

Open your mouth and taste, open your eyes and see— how good GOD is. Blessed are you who run to him. (Psalms 34:8 [MSG])

Example Prayer

Heavenly Father, thank you for creating and shaping me for a purpose and a work. I wholeheartedly believe that you made every part of me perfect.

I affirm that Jesus Christ came with the power to redeem all people. Thank you, Lord Jesus, for redeeming me from eternal death to eternal life.

Holy Spirit, I ask that you redeem my body, starting with my five senses. Please satisfy my eyes because of Christ and let me no longer rely on my natural eyes to find the answer. Instead, open the eyes of my inner self to you, Lord God. Today, I regain my vision, sight, and focus. I ask You, Holy Spirit, to remove the influence of this world that has affected my soul through the lust of the eyes. Cleanse the gates of my eyes, which are the window to the soul, and let my desires be of you and not what I see in the natural. I repent for allowing my eyes to lead me to sin against You. Please forgive me and cleanse me from all unrighteous sight and visions. Purify and refine the gift of sight by Your fire; in Jesus' name, I pray.

I ask You, God, to redeem my tongue and my lying lips; restore my mouth to Your intent when forming them. Let the door of my lips be shut to evil and open to the truth of the spirit. Let the words uttered in my ignorance and sinful state be canceled and removed. I ask that the blood of Jesus Christ be applied to these words. I ask that my words be forgiven, and the consequences of my words canceled and no longer recorded in Heaven. I ask that the fruit of any negative words no longer affect me or others. I humbly ask for forgiveness for my deceitful tongue and pray that my words become righteous and pure before You.

I declare that my soul will no longer have control over my mouth and choose to give the Holy Spirit control over my speech from this day forward. Lord, grant me freedom in speech and boldness to decree your decrees, declare your words, and utter your blessings. I will use my words to defend and protect humanity and to defeat my enemies. I will use my voice to speak God's written and spoken promises and bring them to life in the lives of others, in Jesus' name.

I thank you, God, for teaching my hands to war and my fingers to fight. I will lift my hands to praise your name and to establish your will on earth. Use my hands to build only what you desire. Bless my hands and make them pure and holy so that you will see me each time I lift them up. Allow me to prosper in the works of my hands as I work for your Kingdom, bringing glory and honor to your name, Lord God. Remove every reproach from my hands and burn away lack and poverty from my hands by fire in Jesus' name. Let my hands create, build, and establish greater works in Jesus' name. Anoint my hands to heal the sick, cast out devils, and raise the dead. Anoint my hands to win the battle and overcome the war. Make my hands a sign of victory, just as you did with Moses against the Amalekites. When you hold up my hands, I will not be afraid because you are with me, and I can never fail in you.

Lord God, thank you for giving me a nose to smell. Make me and my life a pleasing aroma and a fragrant offering in your nostrils. Allow all of my senses to work together so that I can discern your heart. Let no smell deceive me like Jacob did Issac when he stole Esau's birthright. Lord God, I ask you to fine-tune all of my natural and spiritual senses according to how you design them to be used.

God, I ask that you give me a hearing heart like Solomon. Please open my spiritual ears to hear on a frequency that aligns with your presence. Remove any ungodly frequencies that have interfered with me hearing your instructions. Remove callouses from my heart so that I can hear and receive you. Protect me from hearing lies and ungodly teachings. Let my ears never be itching for falsehood and unsound doctrine. Close the doors to my ears and soul when doctrines of devils are being spoken, and give me an open ear to your truth, the truth of your Word, and the spirit of truth in Christ Jesus. Give me clarity in what I hear as I press in to listen to your voice, Lord. Jesus said my sheep know my voice and will not follow another one. Let me always hear the voice of Christ Jesus. Holy Spirit, help me to be quick to hear, slow to speak, and slow to anger in Jesus' name. I wear the helmet of salvation and block the voice of anything against your will for my life. Sharpen my ears to hear what the Spirit is saying to the church. Give me acute hearing as I seek to know your heart and your words concerning my prayers. Let me hear and listen to what the Holy Spirit is saying and speak it out by faith. Holy Spirit, activate the hearing *ear and the seeing eye in me so that I may know the will of God, even in the deep things, and be equipped to fulfill my purpose in building the Kingdom of God here on earth.*

Lord God, make every atmosphere I enter submit to the dominion and authority of Christ Jesus. Let every word spoken in my hearing that is not of you be silenced in the name of Jesus Christ. Put a muzzle and a gag on the mouths of evildoers so that they have no voice, no speech, and form no language that I understand. Let the sound of the Heaven where Christ Jesus resides be established in my hearing in Jesus' name, I pray. Amen.

Engaging for Deliverance of Soul, Mind, Will, and Emotions

Now may the God of peace Himself sanctify you completely; and may your whole spirit, soul, and body be preserved blameless at the coming of our Lord Jesus Christ. (1 Thessalonians 5:23)

Example Prayer

Dear Heavenly Father, I come to You today to express my gratitude for creating my mind, will, and emotions. You are the shepherd and bishop of my soul, and I acknowledge that all souls belong to You. I humbly ask that You watch over my soul and keep it in perfect peace. Please fill my soul with joy and make it rich in You.

Clothe my soul with the garments of salvation and the robe of righteousness. I ask You to release me from any soul ties that do not align with Your will for my life. I choose to break, sever, disconnect, and remove all ungodly soul ties, in the name of Jesus Christ, and ask You to establish godly soul ties that will bring blessings into my life. I also pray that You would release my soul from any oaths, inner vows, and curses that would bind me to the lusts of the flesh, the lusts of the eyes, and the pride of life. I receive with humility the grafted word that is able to save my soul. I take authority over my soul and command the release of my soul from manipulation, control, divination, and witchcraft. Let not the enemy persecute my soul, but Lord, restore my soul. Lord, I ask you to keep my soul and deliver me from my enemies. Put to shame those who seek after my soul and rescue my soul from destruction. Let those who seek after my soul be ashamed and confounded and deliver me from all oppressors who seek after my soul. Thank you, Lord, for delivering my soul from death and my feet from falling in Jesus' name. Holy God, I thank you for preserving my soul, for I have been made holy because of Jesus Christ.

Return, O Lord, and deliver my soul, I thank you for causing my soul to rejoice as I lift it up to you. Lord, in patience, I possess my soul. You give comfort to my soul, and it returns to its place of rest in you. I declare that my soul shall live and praise the Lord. Holy Spirit, I ask that you strengthen me with strength in my soul. I proclaim that I will prosper and be in health, even as my soul prospers. I pray that my soul will be preserved blameless unto the coming of the Lord in Jesus' name.

Engaging in Battle
for the Restoration of Our Souls

He refreshes my soul. He guides me along the right paths for his name's sake. (Psalms 23:3)

Example Prayer

Father, we lay at your feet the areas in our hearts that open the door to sickness, disease, and affliction in our minds, will, and emotions. Please shine a light on our emotions today and heal our hearts. Break open every door to our heart that has been closed to the Holy Spirit and restore us so that our bodies can be made whole in you. We ask this in the name of Jesus Christ.

Uproot fear from our hearts and emotions and fill our hearts with the gift of faith. As it says in Hebrews 11:1, "Now faith is the substance of things hoped for, the evidence of things not seen."

Uproot unforgiveness from our hearts and emotions and give us the ability to quickly forgive, for if we do not forgive others their trespasses, neither will you, Father, forgive our trespasses.

Remove the roots of disappointment and bitterness from our hearts and emotions, and give us your grace, God, according to Hebrews 12:15.

We cast all our cares upon you because you care for us; as it says in 1 Peter 5:7, I ask that you uproot the pain of broken hearts today and heal our broken hearts in the name of Jesus, for you heal the brokenhearted and you bind up their wounds, as it says in Psalm 147:3. Repair every breach in our hearts and emotions. Build up the areas that were torn down, build up the walls of our hearts, and secure our hearts with new foundations of your love, joy, and peace in the name of Jesus. See to every cavity in our hearts and excavate. As Proverbs 13:12 says, "Hope deferred makes the heart sick, but when the desire comes, it is a tree of life." For you, oh Lord, are near to those who have a broken heart, and you save those who have a contrite spirit.

Many are the afflictions of the righteous, but the Lord delivers him out of them all. (Psalm 34:19)

In the name of Jesus Christ, we lay at your feet the areas in our minds and thoughts that are compromised and that open the door to sickness, breakdowns, and disease. We decree and declare healing of every broken place in our minds. Heal us from past traumatic experiences and memories that plague our minds and thoughts in the name of Jesus. Re-establish our thoughts and perspectives to see, experience, and remember you: your love, your grace, your mercy, and your favor. We rely on you, Holy Spirit, not our intellect, to determine our thoughts, for you know all things. You tell us to think about whatever is true, whatever is honorable, whatever is just, whatever is pure, whatever is lovely, whatever is commendable, things that are excellent, and things that are worthy of your praise (Philippians 4:8-9).

In the name of Jesus Christ, we command the spirit of worry and anxiety to leave our minds and emotions. We will be anxious for nothing, but in everything, by prayer and supplication, with thanksgiving, we will let our requests be made known to God, and the peace of God, which surpasses all understanding, will guard our hearts and minds through Christ Jesus. (Philippians 4:6-7) Please bring our will, minds, and emotions into balance and agreement with your Holy Spirit in the name of Jesus. A double-minded person is unstable in all their ways. Loose us from all evil influences that operate through our minds and set us free today. Fill us with the mind of Christ Jesus today, for your Word says, "Let this mind be in you which was also in Christ Jesus."

Finally, we pray for restoration in our souls. For you restore our souls and lead us down a path of righteousness for your name's sake (Psalm 23:1-3).

Your Word says, "Beloved, I pray that you may prosper in all things and be in health, just as your soul prospers," (3 John 2). We ask that you repair our souls and cause us to prosper in it in Jesus' name. Jesus, we invite you to sit in the seat of our souls today and direct our minds, will, and emotions in your way by your Holy Spirit. Let your power produce in our lives through the Holy Spirit. We ask all of this in the name of Jesus Christ. Amen.

Engaging the Battle of the Mind

For though we walk in the flesh, we do not war after the flesh: (for the weapons of our warfare are not carnal, but mighty through God to the pulling down of strong holds;) casting down imaginations, and every high thing that exalteth itself against the knowledge of God and bringing into captivity every thought to the obedience of Christ. (2 Corinthians 10:4-5)

Example Prayer

Righteous Defender, we come to you today, having won the victory. Because you love us, I am more than a conqueror against my enemy. I stand in faith that your words are true. I move in confidence that the answer and the solutions for the things that are attacking my mind have already been released into the earth. Mighty God, although I live in this world, my home is in Christ Jesus, who is in

Heaven and not on this earth. I position my spirit in this place of dual citizenship to wage war. I do not wage war as the world does, and I do not use the weapons of this world. I speak your Word, which has divine power to demolish strongholds. I use your Word as a battering axe and to demolish arguments and every accusation that sets itself up against the knowledge of God; I take captive as a son of God every thought and command and its obedience to Christ. I readily punish every place that disobeys your complete Word. I war against the spirit of this age that contends with the knowledge of Christ Jesus and the truth of the Word of God. I bind and take authority over the spirit that intends to blind my mind from the truth, and I declare that I will worship God in spirit and truth. Thank you, God, for training my hands to battle, and now my arms bend stubborn thoughts and strong arguments. I ask you to send your warring angels to arrest and cause every strongman in my mind to be bound and taken to the place of judgment.

Let the blood of the lamb cleanse the battlefield in my mind, and let my thoughts and imagination become the mind of Christ Jesus. My mind is being restored, renewed, and revived as I give myself continually to the Word. Let my mind be peaceful and rest in Jesus' name. Amen.

Engaging in Battle for the Peace of God

Do not be anxious about anything, but in everything, by prayer and petition, with thanksgiving, present your requests to God. And the peace of God, which transcends all understanding, will guard your hearts and your minds in Christ Jesus. (Philippians 4:6-7)

Example Prayer

I pray for peace, Lord God; I pray for your peace to fill our minds in the name of Jesus. I declare Philippians 4:6-7, which says, "Do not be anxious about anything, but in everything, by prayer and petition, with thanksgiving, present your requests to God. And the peace of God, which transcends all understanding, will guard your hearts and your minds in Christ Jesus."

I also pray for peace in my body, spirit, and soul, as Matthew 11:29 tells us, "Take my yoke upon you and learn from me, for I am gentle and humble in heart, and you will find rest for your souls."

May my conversations be filled with peace, and may peace reign in our homes, communities, and workplaces, as I declare 2 Thessalonians 3:16, "Now may the Lord of peace himself give you peace at all times and in every way. The Lord be with all of you." We pray for peace in the body of Christ, as Colossians 3:15 says, "Let the peace of Christ rule in your hearts since as members of one body you were called to peace. And be thankful."

Finally, I pray for peace in my community, knowing that in this world, I will face tribulations, but as John 16:33 reminds me, "I have told you these things, so that in me you may have peace. In this world, you will have trouble. But take heart! I have overcome the world."

Heavenly Father, I put my hope, faith, and trust in You alone. I will rest in Your presence and trust that because You have begun good work for me and my family, You have every situation in the palm of Your hand. I will continue to look to the hills from where my help comes from. I will not rely on what I think or what I know, but I will prove my faith in You by resting on Your promises. I will rest in Your perfect will being done in my life. No one can fight this fight like You.

You, God, know my beginning from my end, and so I will rest in Your faithfulness. Father, friend, and just judge, I ask You to bring every situation into proper alignment with Your will, not my own. I will not lean on my understanding, but I will acknowledge You in all my ways as You direct my path. I choose to make You the author and finisher of my faith. I choose to make You my beginning and my end. I choose to submit to Your sovereignty. I agree with You. I agree with Your will. I agree with Your way. So, I ask that You lift every burden from my mind, will, and emotion. I choose to cast my burdens on You because You care about me. I choose to take Your yoke because it's *easy, and Your burden is light. I rest in You as my Maker, Creator, and God. There is no one like You. I rest in You today, God, and I invite You into everything that concerns me and my family. I lay my head upon Your shoulders, and I rest in You. I cast down my imagination and think of Your promises. I cast down fear and put on Your faith. I cast down anxiety, and I put on Your sufficiency. I cast down doubt, and I put on Your promises. I cast down uncertainty, and I put your assurance on. God, I believe You will not put more on me than I can bear, so I ask for Your supernatural strength to endure this testing until the end.*

Give me the spirit of peace amid upheaval as I look to You as my source, answer, and defender in all things. In Jesus' name, I pray.

I declare Romans 8:35-39, "Who shall separate us from the love of Christ? Shall tribulation, or distress, or persecution, or famine, or nakedness, or peril, or sword? As it is written: "For Your sake, we are killed all day long; We are accounted as sheep for the slaughter." Yet, in all these things, we are more than conquerors through Him who loved us. For I am persuaded that neither death nor life, nor angels nor principalities nor powers, nor things present nor things to come, nor height nor depth, nor any other created thing, shall be able to separate us from the love of God which is in Christ Jesus our Lord.

May the peace of God be with us always, as John 14:27 tells us. Peace you leave with us; the peace you gave us. You do not give as the

world gives, so I will not let our hearts be troubled and will not be
afraid, but I trust you. Amen.

Engaging in Battle
for Faith and Trust in God

Trust in the Lord with all your heart and lean not on your
own understanding; in all your ways submit to him, and he
will make your paths straight. (Proverbs 3:5)

Example Prayer

Thank you, Father, for making the mystery of your will known
to me in prayer, according to the good pleasure which you purposed in
yourself. Thank you, Holy Spirit, for helping me in my times of
weakness; when I am unsure what to pray, you arise in me and
intercede on my behalf. Thank you, Holy Spirit, for searching my
heart and making intercession for me according to the will of God.

Jesus, breathe your breath of life on me and allow me to awake
from my sleep as you come alive in me. Jesus, you paid the ultimate
price and gave your life as a ransom for me so that I may have eternal
and everlasting life. Holy Spirit, quicken this mortal body so I may
live in Christ more abundantly. God, I know that it is impossible to
please you without faith, so I ask that you increase my faith today.
Faith is the substance of things hoped for and the evidence of things
not seen. I apply faith to every area of my life and every situation I

face today. I believe that faith in you, your power, and your love for me will carry me through. Lord God, I believe that without faith, it is impossible to please you, that anyone who comes to you must believe in you, and that you are a rewarder of those who diligently seek you. I choose to seek you diligently today and every day of my life. I receive your promise by faith; I receive your Word by faith; I receive your protection by faith; I receive your grace by faith; I receive your instructions by faith; I receive your direction by faith, and I receive your will by faith in Jesus' name.

Lord God, help me live each day without relying on what I see or think. Nevertheless, I acknowledge you in all my ways and trust in your direction and my path.

Today, God, I trust you with my heart's deep and inner care. I release my fears, inhibitions, worries, doubts, and concerns to you and hold on to your promises. You are faithful, just, everlasting, and kind. As I start my day, I will look to the hills where my help comes from because it comes from you.

I humbly ask you to organize my day and help me prioritize what is important to you. Lord, you are the ruler of my life, so please lead me in the right direction and guide me away from anything wrong in your eyes. I believe that nothing is too hard for you and that nothing can contain or control you. You are the Ancient of Days and the Creator of everything. I submit to your sovereignty and invite you to reign in every aspect of my life. Thank you for your constant love and grace toward me. Keep my feet planted firmly on your foundation as I face every storm and situation. I confidently go through every storm because you have already given me victory. This battle will bring me into a new experience with you. Bring me to your place of awakening and produce in me what is needed to establish your will on the earth. Order my footsteps and the path that I take. I am resolved that you are reshaping the intent of my heart to your intent, and you are ordering my steps, for the steps of a good man are ordered by the Lord. Thank you for being mindful of me, caring about me, and loving me even when I don't know how to love myself. As I seek your face, will, and heart, I know that you are working on my behalf, and so today, I choose to rest in the truth of who and what you are in Jesus' name. Amen.

Engaging in Battle Against My Enemies

According to their deeds, accordingly, He will repay, fury to His adversaries, recompense to His enemies; The coastlands He will fully repay. So shall they fear the name of the Lord from the west, And His glory from the rising of the sun; When the enemy comes in like a flood, The Spirit of the Lord will lift up a standard against him. (Isaiah 59:18-19)

Example Prayer

Jehovah Gibbor, stand against my enemies. Unleash your fiercest weapon and extinguish the fiery darts of the enemy. Cut out of existence the wickedness from around me. Sharpen your sword and fight against those who fight against me and my family. May the disembodied demon spirits operating against me be captured, arrested, and taken to the appointed place of judgment in Jesus' name. Release your sword, mighty God, and slay even the great men and the strong men. Wield your sword against the iron brass and bronze of their city gates. Righteous defender, pour out your indignation as consuming fire. May your wrath be experienced by my enemies. Mighty God, do not keep quiet but repay the wicked and make them as dust that they exist no more. Thank you, mighty warrior and champion, for dealing with my enemies as you did with those who rose against the children of Israel. Lord, shame those who reject you. Let them turn to you and know you are the Most High.

Lord Sabaoth, may the destruction of my enemies be proclaimed in your heavens. LORD of Hosts, separate demons attacking my life from their host in the name of Jesus Christ. Sever the connection of every demon rising against me and call for the angelic assistance assigned to wage war against them in Jesus' name.

May your armies attack the forces of darkness with their weapons of war.

May your judgment stand against them on account of the blood of Jesus Christ over my life now. I am covered with Jesus Christ's blood and righteousness's breastplate.

I use the Word of God to break into pieces invisible chains and restraints and crush the heads of every enemy on assignment against the plan of God for my life this day. I pursue in prayer the gates and territory given to me by God. I identify every unstable foundation in my life, de-throne every idol, false and profane worship, and tear it down in Jesus' name. Holy Spirit, you are the revealer of all things. I call for the exposure of every demonic activity, plan, and plot against me. I call on the Spirit of God to intercept the enemy's plan and bring it to an end. As a son of God on earth, I govern and execute God's jurisdiction and rulership and decree that the law and will of God be manifested in Jesus' name. Release your angels of war that you have given charge over me to engage in this battle on my behalf in Jesus' Name, Amen.

Engaging in Battle
Breaking Fallow Ground

Sow for yourselves righteousness; Reap in mercy; Break up your fallow ground, For it is time to seek the Lord, Till He comes and rains righteousness on you. (Hosea 10:12)

Example Prayer

I plow through every wall, structure, and foundation with the Word of God and shake loose the enemies hold on me in Jesus' name.

I break down every barrier, blockade, and blockage in the spirit, causing delays and hindrances in my life. I command every host being used in every form of iniquity and witchcraft eyes be shut, ears be sealed shut, and hands be bound in Jesus' name. You, God, are the god of peace. You have crushed Satan under my feet. You have delivered my enemy into my hand, and I have been given victory over every adversary.

Thank you for lifting the standard against my enemy when they come in like a flood. I take back by force everything that was stolen from me in the name of Jesus by the authority of the Holy Ghost. I swing my sword, which is the Word of God, and I cut down every stronghold that has tried to control me. I rebuke all demonic agents of authority sent to bring havoc and delay in my life. I break free from every strongman that has tried to bind me. God cancel their assignments and send them to their place of judgment in Jesus' name. I now seal every decree with the blood of Jesus Christ, and thank you, Lord God!

Enduring in Battle

But he who endures to the end shall be saved. (Matthew 24:13)

Example Prayer

Dear Lord, thank you for being my strength, rock, fortress, and deliverer. Because You are my God and my strength, I put my trust in You alone. You are my shield, the horn of my salvation, and my stronghold. Lord, I know You are with me right now, and I am confident You are changing my circumstances for Your glory. Thank you for making my feet like a deer's feet and for giving me the strength to endure to the end so that I might be saved. I decree strength to finish and see the change in me. Thank you for making my enemies my footstool. Thank you for preparing a table before me in the presence of my enemies and for anointing my head with oil as my cup runs over. I now receive the blessing and merit of favor you have given me because I have endured to the end.

Father, you are truth, and your Word is truth. I speak that truth in every area of my life. I bless you for giving me victory over my enemy. Lord, I thank you for making me the head, not the tail, for I know that I am above and not beneath. I am a lender to nations, and my increase is for the Kingdom's building. Thank you for this present situation; I know it is building my faith in You. I know that it is that very faith that helps me to endure to the end and not faint. Lord Jesus,

I trust and believe that all things are working for my good. My faith has brought the things I hoped for to pass this day. I know, Lord, that every day, I am being kept by the power of God through faith unto salvation. Holy Spirit, quicken this mortal body so I may continue fighting this fight of faith. I build myself up now in my most holy faith by praying in your Holy Spirit. Let me know your mind in this situation.

Allow your clarity, revelation, and understanding to be sharpened in me as I pray. May your spirit of discernment increase to a new level so that I may know what is hidden in this situation. In Jesus' name, I pray, amen.

Removal of Rotten Spiritual Roots

Pursue peace with all people, and holiness, without which no one will see the Lord: looking carefully lest anyone fall short of the grace of God; lest any root of bitterness springing up cause trouble, and by this, many become defiled. (Hebrews 12:14-15)

Example Prayer

Because of my act of repentance, in the name of Jesus Christ, I now declare an end to bitterness. May your root be plucked up and removed! I declare an end to rebellion. May your root be plucked up and removed! I declare an end to strife. May your root be plucked up *and removed! I declare an end to control. May your root be plucked up and removed! I declare an end to retaliation. May your root be plucked up and removed! I declare an end to accusations. May your root be plucked up and removed! I declare an end to rejection. May your root be plucked up and removed! I declare an end to insecurity. May your root be plucked up and removed!*

I declare an end to jealousy. May your root be plucked up and removed! I declare an end to withdrawal. May your root be plucked up and removed! I declare an end to escapism. May your root be plucked up and removed! I declare an end to passivity. May your root be plucked up and removed! I declare an end to depression. May your roots be plucked up and removed! I declare an end to heaviness. May your root be plucked up and removed! I declare an end to worry. May your root be plucked up and removed! I declare an end to nervousness. May your root be plucked up and removed! I declare an end to sensitiveness. May your root be plucked up and removed! I declare an end to persecution. May your root be plucked up and removed! I declare an end to mental illness. May your roots be plucked up and removed! I declare an end to schizophrenia & paranoia. May your roots be plucked up and removed! I declare an end to confusion. May your root be plucked up and removed! I declare an end to pride. May your root be plucked up and removed! I declare an end to grief. May your root be plucked up and removed! I declare an end to the confusion. May your root be plucked up and removed! I declare an end to doubt. May your root be plucked up and removed! I declare an end to indecision. May your root be plucked up and removed! I declare an end to false identity. May your root be plucked up and removed! I declare an end to greediness. May your root be plucked up and removed! I declare an end to perfection. May your root be plucked up and removed! I declare an end to self-deception. May your root be plucked up and removed! I declare an end to mind binding, so may your root be plucked up and removed! I declare an end to mind idolatry, and may your root be plucked up and removed! I declare an end to fear, and may your root be plucked up and removed! I declare an end to the fear of authority. May your root be plucked up and removed! I declare an end to perfection. May your root be plucked up and removed! I declare an end to competition. May your root be plucked up and removed! I declare an end to impatience. May your root be plucked up and removed! I declare an end to false burdens. May your root be plucked up and removed! I declare an end to fatigue. May your root be plucked up and removed! I declare an end to infirmities. May your root be plucked up and removed! I declare an end to death. May your root be plucked up and removed! I declare an end to hyperactivity. May your root be plucked up and removed! I declare an end to cursing. May your root be plucked up and removed! I declare an end to addictive compulsiveness. May your root be plucked up and removed!

I declare an end to gluttony. May your root be plucked up and removed! I declare an end to self-accusation. May your root be plucked up and removed! I declare an end to guilt. May your root be plucked up and removed! I declare an end to perversion. May your root be plucked up and removed! I declare an end to false and profane worship. May your root be plucked up and removed! I declare an end to false religions, occults, and religiosity. May your root be plucked up and removed in Jesus' name. Holy God, I ask that you send your angels to gather every root that was removed by your holy spirit and burn them by fire in Jesus' name I pray, Amen.

Resting in the Confidence of God

In the fear of the Lord, there is strong confidence, and His children will have a place of refuge. (Proverbs 14:26)

Example Prayer

Gracious God, you are my Redeemer. When the enemy came in like a flood, Your Spirit lifted a standard against him, and I thank You for this. Thank You, Lord, for returning, delivering, and saving me from all those who persecuted me. Thank You, Lord, for being a shield to me. You are the one who lifted my head. I was unafraid of ten thousand people who set themselves against me because I knew you would deliver me. You have not given me the spirit of fear but of love, power, and a sound mind. I use these gifts as I take an offensive

146

posture against every demonic manifestation. Thank you for vindicating me against false accusers and fulfilling your promise.

Only You, Lord God, have rained coal, fire, brimstone, and a burning wind against my enemy. Lord, I rest in You, knowing that You are God. You are exalted among the nations and the earth. Father God, I pray today that the words of my mouth and the meditation of my heart be acceptable in Your sight, oh Lord, my strength and my Redeemer. Father, I know my tongue is the pen of a ready writer. I write the blessings that You have declared in my life into existence now in the name of Jesus. Great Jehovah, I speak to every mountain that is an obstacle in my life and command it by faith to move. Lord God, I thank You for giving me the tongue of the learned so that I may speak Your Word in and out of season. I declare the Word of God that in blessing, You have blessed me and kept me because I am the righteousness of God. I am not forsaken, and my seed will never beg for bread. I declare the works of my hands are blessed. I proclaim peace, love, prosperity, and goodness in Jesus' name. Amen.

About the Author

Natassia K. Blassingame is the Pastor of Worldwide Empowerment Center, Inc., located in Wyomissing, PA. She is known as the "Igniter" for her fervent prayer, prophecy, and preaching, and she is a sought-after preacher, teacher, and Kingdom strategist. Founder of My Sister's Keeper, she empowers women and communities, addressing issues like homelessness, addiction, and teen pregnancy. Natassia lives with her husband, Bishop Corey J. Blassingame Sr., their three children, and two grandchildren.

Description

Acts of War: A Strategic Prayer Manual for Believers by Natassia K. Blassingame is a guide for deepening prayer lives and advancing authority in Christ. It equips readers with practical tools for spiritual warfare, fostering community in the shared spiritual battle, and empowering believers to integrate meaningful prayer into daily life.

Published by:

A division of LifeSpring Publishing

www.scrollpublishers.com

Has God spoken to you about writing a book?

Let us help you!

www.ingramcontent.com/pod-product-compliance
Lightning Source LLC
LaVergne TN
LVHW011330080426
835513LV00006B/270